Foreword

Clive is a student of the Word and th[...]
an excellent job of providing 'capsules of revelation' and
practical steps for financial health and prosperity. His focus
on the purpose of money and the steps that acknowledge
that purpose, provide any believer with a 'track' for changing
their lives. In a world that is full of economic uncertainty and
the life-strangling fear that accompanies such uncertainty,
Clive provides from the Word of God, the unshakeable
principles that anchor our lives.

Already before this book was written numerous families
have benefitted greatly from the teaching in it. As you read
this book, the Holy Spirit comes to ignite your faith and
speak into your heart. You will rise from whatever your
financial state is currently to a new place of being debt-free,
possessing financial stability and certainty. Your 'abundant
life,' promised by Scripture, is advanced as you actually
apply what you read. Move out of financial paralysis into
Kingdom blessing by stepping on the 'escalator of blessing'
provided by the tracks of this book.

Rick Johnston
Pastor of New Life Bible Church, Harrow

Contents

Preface

It was April 2016. My wife and I had sat down together and had drawn up a list of things we wanted to purchase and do. They included buying a tent so we could go to a Christian camping event, a shed to store our tools which were getting damaged, a holiday, new windows and doors for parts of the house which were not doing a great job of keeping the cold winter air out of the house. We also had computers that had stopped working or were seriously playing up. I was trying to work out how I could manage to afford all of these things. It is amazing how much pressure you can feel trying to work out your own finances. I came to the conclusion that I could only do this with a bonus (and a sizeable one at that). Bonus time was the end of April and so I waited with anticipation for the announcement. The announcement came on time - no bonus!

It was at this time that God was talking to me about the passage from Matthew 14:13-21 and was revealing to me keys to living in divine provision. To cut a long story short, within 9 months of implementing these principles, we now give at least 27% of our income (which is rising all the time), we are paying off our debt at an accelerated rate. Our list of things we needed or wanted have been almost completely met. I am now working less hard than I did before but seeing increased reward for that work. In short, we have moved from an unhealthy place to a lot healthier place.

I have also applied these principles to a number of people who are struggling with their finances. A selection of their stories are found in the testimonies section of this book at Appendix 6. I have seen time after time God working in their lives to bring supernatural increase and provision. What I have discovered is that when you apply the principles of God's kingdom, whatever your situation, they will work!

As a result, the aim of this book is simple yet huge. To create a generation of God's people who are empowered to live and prosper in financial freedom and fulfil their purpose and calling to give generously and outrageously in order to see the kingdom of God advance.

Whilst this book will definitely give you step by step advice on how to change your financial situation, it aims to do a lot more than this. It aims to free a generation of God's people into their purpose and identity in Him. As believers, we have a limited amount of time on this earth and are limited in energy, yet we have access to the unlimited resources of heaven. So often though I see believers exhausting what is limited (their time and energy) to access what is unlimited (provision). This is clearly the wrong way round, the unlimited resources of heaven are designed to be accessed so that you can use your time and energy for eternal purposes.

If you read, pray and follow the practical exercises, over 40 days you will grasp God's heart for your finances, you will understand and embrace your purpose, you will take control of your money, you will be empowered to get out of debt and you will understand and be able to implement the keys to financial increase.

May the Lord bless you richly as you read this book.

Day 1 - God's Heart for Your Finances

"And God is able to bless you abundantly, so that in all things at all times, having all that you need, you will abound in every good work." 2 Corinthians 9:8

This verse summarises God's heart for your finances. God wants to bless you abundantly.   Abundantly means you will have more than enough.

God wants to give you more than enough in "all things". This covers your house, your food, your clothes, your hobbies, your passions - in short when he says "all things" he means "all things".

Also God wants to bless you at "all times". There are not seasons when God wants to bless you. He wants to bless you all the time. There should not be one second where you are without the blessing of God.

God wants you to have all that you need. There should be no lack, no poverty, no time or period where you are lacking any good thing.   Poverty is not a sign of godliness - in the Old Testament poverty was clearly labelled a curse.

The reason why God wants you to have more than enough is so that you can "abound in every good work". The blessing on your life is so that you have enough for yourself and enough to give away to others. He wants your life so full that you are ready at any time, in any area of your life, to bless others around you. God's blessings are never just for you, they are always so that you are able to bless others. This is why a lifestyle which lusts after money and material goods is also not what God has for us.

Yet this verse says that God is "able". This means that God has the ability to bless you in this way BUT NOT that he automatically does so.

Jesus always spoke about the kingdom of God. One of the best known examples of when Jesus spoke about the kingdom of God was in the "Lord's Prayer". The Lord's

6

Prayer contains an important line "Your kingdom come, your will be done on earth as it is in heaven". God wants his kingdom, as demonstrated in heaven, to be replicated on the earth. A "kingdom" is the dominion of a king. In other words the area of influence of a king. God wants his dominion and influence to be present on our earth. Kingdoms have laws and rules. God's kingdom is no different - his kingdom has rules and laws. If you want God to bless you abundantly you need to understand and implement the rules of His kingdom.

Over 40 days, we will set out the key principles and laws of God's kingdom as they relate to finances. I have broken these key principles into 4 distinct sections:

1.   understanding why God has given you money;
2.   stewarding what you have through wisdom;
3.   exercising faith to meet your needs; and
4.   principles for increase.

Throughout the chapters of this book we will explore these rules of His kingdom and see the keys to living this life of abundance or "more than enough" which is available to believers.

Question:

Have you ever thought about what abundance looks like? What do you think abundance looks like for you?

Practical Exercise

Take some time to dream with God. Think about what you would do if you lived in abundance and fill in this table with your dreams:

Area	Dream
Giving	
Living - where/what kind of accommodation	
Special Dreams - car/holiday etc.	
Investments	
Inheritance	
Debt	
God Dreams	
Calling - what has God called you to do - what resources do you need?	

SECTION 1 - WHY HAS GOD GIVEN ME MONEY?

Day 2 - The Primary Purpose for Your Money

Many Christians do not understand why God gives us money. If we do not understand the primary purpose for the money we handle, we can never truly enter into the full level of blessing and abundance that God has for us. As a father, I would not trust my daughter with a bread knife until she knew what it was meant for and was mature enough to handle it. Why? She may well hurt herself! Our loving father is exactly the same when it comes to money, which if used foolishly, can destroy our life. He wants us to know what it is for and how to handle it.

The primary purpose for money was addressed by Jesus in one of the most difficult parables to understand. It is found in Luke 16:1-13:

"Jesus told his disciples: "There was a rich man whose manager was accused of wasting his possessions. So he called him in and asked him, 'What is this I hear about you? Give an account of your management, because you cannot be manager any longer.'
"The manager said to himself, 'What shall I do now? My master is taking away my job. I'm not strong enough to dig, and I'm ashamed to beg— I know what I'll do so that, when I lose my job here, people will welcome me into their houses.'
"So he called in each one of his master's debtors. He asked the first, 'How much do you owe my master?'
"'Nine hundred gallons of olive oil,' he replied.
"The manager told him, 'Take your bill, sit down quickly, and make it four hundred and fifty.'
"Then he asked the second, 'And how much do you owe?'
"'A thousand bushels of wheat,' he replied.
"He told him, 'Take your bill and make it eight hundred.'
"The master commended the dishonest manager because he had acted shrewdly. For the people of this world are more shrewd in dealing with their own kind than are the people of the light. I tell you, use worldly wealth to gain

friends for yourselves, so that when it is gone, you will be welcomed into eternal dwellings.

"Whoever can be trusted with very little can also be trusted with much, and whoever is dishonest with very little will also be dishonest with much. So if you have not been trustworthy in handling worldly wealth, who will trust you with true riches? And if you have not been trustworthy with someone else's property, who will give you property of your own?

"No one can serve two masters. Either you will hate the one and love the other, or you will be devoted to the one and despise the other. You cannot serve both God and money."

The Meaning

In order to understand this parable and the important message that Jesus is trying to convey, we need to understand who the characters in the story represent:

The Rich Man - he represents God. The rich man owns everything that the manager is managing. In the same way everything in this planet belongs to God (see Psalm 24:1 *"The earth is the Lord's, and everything in it, the world, and all who live in it"*). There is nothing that God does not own.

The Manager - he represents us. Each of us have been given money to manage by God. This money is not ours - we are merely given it to steward or manage. Some get to manage a lot, others less. In the same way as the manager was going to lose his job managing the rich man's assets, all of us will one day die and when we die our assignment of managing God's money will also end. As the manager had squandered some of the rich man's assets, we also are likely to have been guilty of mishandling God's money.

The Debtors - are the people who do not know Jesus. Sin is described as a debt that cannot be repaid. So the rich man's debtors represent those who have sinned against God.

So what does the story mean? The manager used the rich man's money and gave it away to people who owed his master money. He gave the money away to gain influence with his debtors so that when he lost his job, those debtors would look favourably on him and look after him. Amazingly the master applauded the manager!

Why did the master applaud the manager? It is because when the manager was generous to the master's creditors, he was acting on behalf of the master. The master looked good because of what the manager was doing. He appeared to be kind and generous.

As managers of God's money, we are to use that money to gain influence with those who are lost in order to bring them into the kingdom of God. This is why Jesus says to use worldly wealth to win friends for yourselves who will greet you when you go to heaven. The picture here is that we will be greeted by those who we have won to Jesus through careful use of our money.

How does using our money in this way reflect the character of God? It represents Him as both kind and generous (which He is!). So every time we give, we reflect the nature of our God to a world lost in materialism and selfishness.

Non-christians understand the power of money in opening up people's lives. This is why businessmen will spend money in buying meals in order to open doors to new business. They will send gifts in order to strengthen business relationships. The world is more shrewd than the Church because they understand the power of money.

Money is neither good nor bad - yet it does have power. Jesus is urging believers to use money to influence non-believers and win them for the kingdom. An example of this would be my friend Robert. It was 1989 and Robert had just taken £10 out of a cash machine. He was walking through the London Underground at Marble Arch and saw a girl who appeared to be either drunk or high on drugs who was begging for money. Robert passed by the girl and immediately thought to give her the money, but as it was all the money he had on him and as he wanted to spend it on himself, he carried on walking. Yet as he walked away from the girl, his heart became heavy. God spoke to Robert and said "give that girl your £10". Robert was not happy. Why should he give this girl his £10 when she was clearly going to spend it on something which was no good for her? However, Robert was obedient. He walked back to the girl and gave her the £10. However, as Robert was not happy about giving the money, he thought that he was not going to let her get away without a message. So he said "More than you need this (the £10.00 note), you need Jesus". As Robert would admit, this was not said with a good heart but out of frustration. When she saw the note her eyes came in focus and she became alert for a second. Robert then turned and left at a pace. He did not want a conversation as he was unhappy and grumpy that he had given all the money he had just taken out, to spend on himself.

A number of years later, Robert was attending a Christian meeting and saw the same girl recalling her testimony of how she got saved. The girl recounted that one day she was high and begging on the London Underground. She remembers very clearly a man giving her £10 and telling her that "More than you need this, you need Jesus". Those words haunted her and she could not let them go. When a friend invited her to go to church, she was keen to do so in order to discover who this Jesus was. She went off to find out about this God who loved her enough to give her money and share a message.

That story never ceases to amaze me. Could there ever be a better investment, £10 to see a soul know Jesus? God was happy to take even a grumpy message combined with obedience in the area of money as a seed to bring a precious soul to salvation. As believers we have the fantastic opportunity to give to missionaries who devote their lives to bringing the good news. We can give to church organisations who are looking to expand the kingdom. We can give to those who serve us in restaurants a huge tip with a message of how much God loves them. All of these are designed at seeing souls saved and the kingdom of God advance.

Note that the manager does not give away the same amount to each person who owes his master money. Some he cuts their debt by 50% others by 20%. The manager is choosing which of his master's creditors are most likely to help him in the future. In the same way we are to be wise in our giving. We are looking to maximise the return on our investment as we hear the voice of the Lord to give.

Prayer

"Father, I am sorry for the times I have lived my life without reference to your plans and purpose for my money. Today I declare that I have decided to pursue my primary purpose for money and give generously and outrageously to the kingdom of God. Please give me wisdom and faith for this journey"

Questions

If I were to look at your spending patterns, would I see evidence that you were pursuing the primary purpose of God for your money? Why?

Practical Application

What would your bank account look like if you were pursuing your primary purpose? How much would you give and how much would you spend?

Pray about this question with God and allow the Holy Spirit to speak to you in this area.

Day 3 - The Money Test

"Whoever can be trusted with very little can also be trusted with much, and whoever is dishonest with very little will also be dishonest with much. So if you have not been trustworthy in handling worldly wealth, who will trust you with true riches? And if you have not been trustworthy with someone else's property, who will give you property of your own? "No one can serve two masters. Either you will hate the one and love the other, or you will be devoted to the one and despise the other. You cannot serve both God and money." Luke 16

Today we continue with Luke 16.

The Test

Jesus says if we can trusted in little we can trusted in much. If we can use the money we steward for God for its primary purpose, to see the kingdom of God advance and win souls, then we qualify to be trusted with more. This certainly includes more money, but is certainly not limited to money and material wealth.

Whilst so many believers want to be given a larger money assignment from God, what they fail to realise is that they have to pass the test attached to their current money assignment! Pursuing God's purpose for your money is critical to seeing increase.

Yet if we do not use our money for its primary purpose, Jesus describes this as being "dishonest" with your money. You do not qualify for more.

If you are trustworthy in using your "worldly wealth" for the primary purpose of the kingdom, then you qualify for "true riches". This is not diamonds or gold! True riches are things of eternal consequence, such as the gifts of God, the opportunity to bless others and see them come to salvation and even revival itself.   If we only realised what could be achieved by managing our money with God's purposes in mind.

Money is always a test. Yet it is the key to "true riches". There has never been more at stake. Never has any test had such serious repercussions.

The Battle for Your Service

Jesus concludes this lesson with the warning "you cannot serve both God and money". The NIV version of the bible does not accurately reflect what Jesus is saying here. What Jesus is actually saying is that "you cannot serve both God and **Mammon**". What is Mammon? Mammon is an Assyrian God of money and wealth. It is a demonic power which sits behind money. Mammon seeks to replace God.

What Jesus is saying is that you can only hold onto God or Mammon. They are mutually exclusive. You can only hold onto one of them - you need to choose! This is not surprising when you realise that Mammon is a demonic power. You must choose between God and a demon.

How does Mammon effect us? Well let's start with why people want money.

People want money because they believe:

1.   it gives you power;
2.   it gives you status;
3.   it gives you security; and
4.   it gives you provision.

We have all seen movies, adverts and media which all underline the importance of money. Yet so many of us inadvertently buy into this belief system.

There are many ways in which Mammon can influence our lives:

1. **Big Spenders** - these people buy things to make themselves feel important or powerful. They gain status and importance through buying things.

2. **Hoarders** - these people find security in having lots of things. Their house is full of stuff and in the clutter security is found.

3. **Proud savers** - these people have spent a lifetime to create a nest egg. They have sacrificed a lot in order to create their safety net. Their security is found in those savings.

4. **Greedy** - life is defined by how much I own. There is never enough there is constant discontent with where you are. Money is status and having money and the trappings of money lets everyone know how important you are. Their status is found in the money.

Yet as believers, God is my provider. God is my strong tower and my security. God tells me I am His son adopted into His family - this is my status. God gives us authority and power. God is the real thing - Mammon is the counterfeit.

Mammon is in direct competition to replace God in your life. This is why you cannot hold on to God and also hold on to money. You must make the choice as to who you rely on for your power, status, security and provision.

God is willing to give you money so long as money never claims your heart.

Yet money often pulls on our heart. I find this happens most when a sudden bill comes in or an unexpected expense.

There is a fear that grips my heart that pushes me to try to control my finances. It affects my mood and I am suddenly thinking about how I can hold onto money in different ways. I have learned to recognise that that feeling is the effect of mammon on my life trying to control me. I have unconsciously brought into the lie that money is my security and that I can control my security. It is important that we learn to discern when Mammon is trying to control our lives.

That fear wants to control me and my life and if I let it, it will do just that. I have learnt that the best cure for that fear is to give more extravagantly than before! Nothing breaks that fear and control faster.

Questions

Does Mammon have a control in your life? If so in what way?

Do you identify with the big spenders, the hoarders, the proud savers or the greedy? Why is this?

What do you think you can you do to break the power of mammon in your life?

Prayer

"Lord, I choose you not Mammon. I ask for grace to change my heart attitude to money. I run to you and hold onto you and at the same time I let go of Mammon. I love you Lord above everything else!!"

Day 4 - Decide Where Your Treasure Lies

"Do not store up for yourselves treasures on earth, where moths and vermin destroy, and where thieves break in and steal. But store up for yourselves treasures in heaven, where moths and vermin do not destroy, and where thieves do not break in and steal. For where your treasure is, there your heart will be also.

"The eye is the lamp of the body. If your eyes are healthy, your whole body will be full of light. But if your eyes are unhealthy, your whole body will be full of darkness. If then the light within you is darkness, how great is that darkness!

"No one can serve two masters. Either you will hate the one and love the other, or you will be devoted to the one and despise the other. You cannot serve both God and money."
Matt 6:19-24

You will see immediately that the passage in Matt 6 (above) concludes in verse 24 with the same verse as we read in Luke 16. You cannot serve God and Mammon. You have to make a choice. This is Jesus repeating the same thought he expressed in Luke 16, but in a different context. Whenever Jesus repeats himself, it is usually because what he was saying was of particular importance and he didn't want his disciples to miss the message he was giving.

Today we are going to explore what Jesus is saying in these verses.

He starts off with a command "do not store up treasures on earth" but instead "store up for yourselves treasures in heaven". Storing up treasures on earth is easy to understand. He is saying do not make the accumulation of wealth your priority in life, as it will not last. Instead, we are to make our priority storing treasures up in heaven. How do we store up treasures in heaven?

In Matthew 19:21, Jesus spells it out when he says to a young ruler: ""*If you want to be perfect, go, sell your possessions and give to the poor, and you will have **treasure in heaven**. Then come, follow me.*"" Jesus is saying that selling possessions and giving them to the poor will result in treasures in heaven. In other words generosity will result in treasures in heaven.

Again the phrase treasures in heaven is used in Luke 19:33 which reads: "*Sell your possessions and give to the poor. Provide purses for yourselves that will not wear out, a **treasure in heaven that will never fail,** where no thief comes near and no moth destroys.*"

In 1 Tim 6:18-19 we read *"Command them to do good, to be rich in good deeds, and to be generous and willing to share. In this way they will lay up **treasure** for themselves as a firm foundation for the coming age, so that they may take hold of the life that is truly life"*.

The message from scripture is clear, treasures in heaven occur when we are being generous. It is a shift in focus from making your own comfort and wealth the priority to looking out for the needs of others. This is the primary purpose for your money - to give generously to see the kingdom of God expand.

Jesus then says "*The eye is the lamp of the body. If your eyes are healthy, your whole body will be full of light. But if your eyes are unhealthy, your whole body will be full of darkness. If then the light within you is darkness, how great is that darkness!*" This verse is also connected to this issue of money.

The eye is likened to the lamp of the body. The purpose of

a lamp is simple: it produces light. If I have a lamp which stops producing light, it is useless to me as its purpose is to produce light. What Jesus is saying is that our eyes (or in particular what we focus on with our eyes) is supposed to produce light for our body.

What Jesus is saying is that when our focus is healthy then our whole body will be full of light. What does Jesus mean by light? Scripture is filled references to light and darkness. The very first words spoken by God were "let there be light". God declares then that the light was good. Light represents a life lived to its fullest in accordance with God's plans and promises. This is why the prophet Isaiah declared about Jesus "the people have seen a great light". So when the focus and purpose of our life is healthy then our whole life will be full of God's life and promises.

What does Jesus mean by saying our eyes must be "healthy"? The Greek word for "healthy" implies generous. So what Jesus is saying is that when the focus of our life is generosity then our life will be full of God's life and promises.

By contrast, if our eyes are unhealthy, or stingy, then our life will not be full of light but instead will be full of darkness. We will live without the life of God in our lives. We will live not knowing the fullness of what God has for us. So if the focus of our eyes is on what makes us more comfortable or happy and not on blessing others with generosity then our life will be without hope and fullness.

Jesus concludes this thought by saying "*If then the light within you is darkness, how great is that darkness!*" Your eyes are supposed to be a lamp to light your body. If your eyes are not producing that light because they are focused on your own pleasures then it is like being blind. The darkness we live in when our source of light has been extinguished will be great.

So Jesus again puts the choice to us. We can serve money and put our focus on our own wealth and comfort or we can live a life of purpose and generosity. We can embrace Mammon and live a life of darkness or we can live a life of generosity, giving extravagantly to the kingdom of God and live in glorious light. We can store up treasures on this earth or we can give generously and store up treasures in heaven.

Our life will be defined by whether or not we love money or God. There has never been a more difficult or important test.

Prayer

"Father, my heart is to pursue my purpose in life - to give generously to your kingdom. Please give me grace and wisdom to pursue you".

Day 5- Embracing your purpose brings you into provision

"And why do you worry about clothes? See how the flowers of the field grow. They do not labor or spin. Yet I tell you that not even Solomon in all his splendor was dressed like one of these. If that is how God clothes the grass of the field, which is here today and tomorrow is thrown into the fire, will he not much more clothe you—you of little faith? So do not worry, saying, 'What shall we eat?' or 'What shall we drink?' or 'What shall we wear?' For the pagans run after all these things, and your heavenly Father knows that you need them. But seek first his kingdom and his righteousness, and all these things will be given to you as well." Matthew 6:28-33

The message of this passage is clear. If we pursue God's kingdom, then our needs will be met by God. As we pursue God's purpose for our money in giving to see the kingdom of God grow, God will look after us and provide for us. If we care about what God cares about, he will care for us. I would much rather God look after me rather than rely on my own resources.

I have seen the truth of this passage on many occasions. For those who are willing to take a risk and trust God's word, the results are always the same. God always comes through. There was one lady living on very little money. I went through her finances with her and challenged her to trust God in the area of giving to him. At the time she had debts which she had no way of repaying. When she gave money from her income to God, within a week she had received a refund from the government for discretionary compensation. She was able to use this to pay her debts. Embracing your purpose opens up the doors of provision in your life.

Jesus told a famous parable of the lost son. Many people rightly see this parable as being all about the outrageous love of a father. However, this parable also has a money message in it.

Luke 15:11 *"Jesus continued: "There was a man who had two sons. The younger one said to his father, 'Father, give* me my share of the estate.' So he divided his property between them. Not long after that, the younger son got together all he had, set off for a distant country and there squandered his wealth in wild living. After he had spent everything, there was a severe famine in that whole country, and he began to be in need. So he went and hired himself out to a citizen of that country, who sent him to his fields to feed pigs. He longed to fill his stomach with the pods that the pigs were eating, but no one gave him anything. "When he came to his senses, he said, 'How many of my father's hired servants have food to spare, and here I am starving to death! I will set out and go back to my father and say to him: Father, I have sinned against heaven and against you. I am no longer worthy to be called your son; make me like one of your hired servants.' So he got up and went to his father."But while he was still a long way off, his father saw him and was filled with compassion for him; he ran to his son, threw his arms around him and kissed him. The son said to him, 'Father, I have sinned against heaven and against you. I am no longer worthy to be called your son.' "But the father said to his servants, 'Quick! Bring the best robe and put it on him. Put a ring on his finger and sandals on his feet. Bring the fattened calf and kill it. Let's have a feast and celebrate. For this son of mine was dead and is alive again; he was lost and is found.' So they began to celebrate. "Meanwhile, the older son was in the field. When he came near the house, he heard music and dancing. So he called one of the servants and asked him what was going on. Your brother has come,' he replied, 'and your father has killed the fattened calf because he has him back safe and sound.'"The older brother became angry and refused to go in. So his father went out and pleaded with him. But he answered his father, 'Look! All these years I've been slaving for you and never disobeyed your orders. Yet you never gave me even a young goat so I could celebrate with my friends. But when this son of yours who has squandered your property with prostitutes comes home, you kill the fattened calf for him!'" 'My son,' the father said, 'you are always with me, and everything I have is yours. But we had to celebrate and be glad, because this brother of yours was dead and is alive again; he was lost and is found.' "

The Sons and the Father

The parable is all about two sons and a father. God declares that we are His adopted sons (Eph 1:5). This parable can be applied to us. The sons' job was to work in the father's house and working in the father's business. In the same way, as we explored in the previous days, we are to work in the father's business of expanding His kingdom.

Whilst the sons were at home working for the father, they were provided for in terms of accommodation, food, clothes etc. When we work for the father in seeking first His kingdom, we get to enjoy the promise of provision (see Matthew 6 above).

The Money Test

Yet the younger son decided he wanted to take control of his financial future. He effectively said to his father, "I wish you were dead so I can have my inheritance". He had no desire to pursue his father's business - his focus was selfish and concentrated only on his own plans. He didn't realise that his assignment was to steward his father's wealth. Instead, he wanted wealth of his own. His thinking was short term - he didn't realise that by working for his father, he was in fact protecting and increasing his inheritance so that when his father died he would inherit even more.

In the same way, as believers, we can so easily forget God's plan for our finances. We can focus on our own short term plans which are separate from God's purpose for our money. We can become both selfish and very short sighted.

Money Outside of Purpose

The son takes his money out of his father's house and the bible says he squandered it in wild living. As believers, we need to realise that the moment we take our money outside of God's purpose of building His kingdom it is squandered. It has no eternal consequence and more than that, it is likely to disappear.

The younger son is then forced to work in a pig farm - there was probably no more demeaning work for a Jewish man.

Outside of the Father's House there was no provision, instead the son had to take demeaning work just to survive. When we take money and fail to use it for kingdom purposes we have made life hard for ourselves - we have chosen to rely on our own resources. This will ultimately result in us trying to sustain ourselves.

The Road back to the Father

The bible said that the younger son "came to his senses". In other words, the younger son readjusted his attitude. He was willing to embrace an assignment as a servant to his father. He gave up his "rights" realising that simply being in the Father's house was better than living in his own strength If we have been using our wealth for us, not Him, we need to have an attitude readjustment. Are we willing to serve God by stewarding our money for kingdom increase?

The son came back willing to serve his father. His father saw him and ran to him giving up his pride, his status and his right to be offended. This is the father we have. Whatever mess we have made of our financial assignments, the moment we come back to him with an attitude of service, our God will run to us with open arms. Do we deserve it? Definitely not! This is the beauty of grace.

Not only did the father run to the son, but gave him valuable gifts and a public party to affirm not his position as a servant but as a son. A ring of authority and a robe. This is our God. He is longing to reaffirm our sonship by publicly blessing us with gifts and favour.

The Older Son

The older brother was not happy to see his younger brother. He was even less happy that the younger son was being blessed in a public setting. His words to his father reflect his attitude. He said "I've been slaving for you". The older son completely misunderstood his assignment. He was working for his father to increase his inheritance. Yet he called this slavery. How wrong could he be?

There are so many Christians that see giving to the kingdom as "slavery". Something they have to do but they don't want to do. 'I give money to the church because my pastor says I must!" How wrong can we be? Do we not realise that embracing God's purpose for our life positions us for increase and true riches?

The father corrected the older son's view. Everything that he owned now belonged to the older son. It is exactly the same for us as believers (see 2 Peter 1:3) - God has given us all things. Yet as believers, we often live as if this were not true. Like the older son we need to soften our hearts and listen to the voice of God as he guides us and loves us.

Conclusion

As believers we get the opportunity to step into the provision of God by embracing His mission and His purpose. A life outside of God's purpose is wasted.

Questions?

Are you living like the younger son by using money for whatever you want and ignoring the assignment of God? If so, why do you think this is?

Are you living like the older son - only giving because you are required to? If so, why do you think this is?

Prayer

"Lord, I commit myself to serving you. I want to be in your house, serving your purposes. I trust that as I serve you, you will provide for me, not just what I need but also so much more.

Lord, I am sorry where I have used my money outside of your purpose. I am also sorry where I have treated serving you as a chore. I want to know the joy of service every day"

Day 6 - The Rewards of Service

Our next money parable is not a parable you would normally consider to be a money parable! It is the parable of the good Samaritan. In Luke 10:25, Jesus tells the following parable:

"On one occasion an expert in the law stood up to test Jesus. "Teacher," he asked, "what must I do to inherit eternal life?" "What is written in the Law?" he replied. "How do you read it?" He answered, "'Love the Lord your God with all your heart and with all your soul and with all your strength and with all your mind'; and, 'Love your neighbor as yourself.'" You have answered correctly," Jesus replied. "Do this and you will live." But he wanted to justify himself, so he asked Jesus, "And who is my neighbor?" In reply Jesus said: "A man was going down from Jerusalem to Jericho, when he was attacked by robbers. They stripped him of his clothes, beat him and went away, leaving him half dead. A priest happened to be going down the same road, and when he saw the man, he passed by on the other side. So too, a Levite, when he came to the place and saw him, passed by on the other side. But a Samaritan, as he traveled, came where the man was; and when he saw him, he took pity on him. He went to him and bandaged his wounds, pouring on oil and wine. Then he put the man on his own donkey, brought him to an inn and took care of him. The next day he took out two denarii and gave them to the innkeeper. 'Look after him,' he said, 'and when I return, I will reimburse you for any extra expense you may have.' "

The clear message of this parable is about loving your neighbour. However, there is a money element to this parable.

The Good Samaritan in the parable can represent Jesus. He helps a man who is robbed, beaten and left for dead. It is the Devil's job to kill, steal and destroy lives (see John 10:10) - he represents the robber. The man whose life has been destroyed by the robbers represents a person whose life is destroyed by the works of the Devil. Jesus comes to rescue those who have been attacked by the Devil. He heals the brokenhearted and binds up their wounds (Ps 147:3). He applies the oil of the spirit and the wine is a reference to the power of His blood.

Then where does Jesus take the man who has been attacked? He takes him to an Inn. What does the Inn represent? It represents the church. God uses His church to care for those who have been rescued by Jesus.

This is where the parable then takes on a money angle. The good Samaritan gives the Innkeeper money and promises more money in the future. From the innkeeper's point of view, he is looking after the man because he is expecting to make a profit (or reward) on his services. If we apply this to the church, Jesus is willing to profit or reward us for looking after those who have been saved. Whether it is teaching them, housing them, giving generously to them, standing by them in difficult situations etc. Yet as believers, we simply say "no thanks - I do this because I love Jesus". There is much to commend this attitude. We do not serve God for selfish reasons. Yet we miss a critical attribute of God - he is a rewarder.

Now reward must be properly understood. We never work for our salvation or favour from God. These are free gifts of God. We work from a place of favour. Yet the nature of any father is to bless their children when they are doing well or when they display the character we are looking to see.

This is what Jesus meant as reward. As a father I love my children unconditionally. Yet I have learned only to reward them when they show good character traits (such as honesty, kindness or simply trying their best) - or else they will develop behaviours and attitudes which can be unhealthy. Why do we think our heavenly father is any different? We access everything in the kingdom of God through faith. In Hebrews 11:6, the bible says "And without faith it is impossible to please God, because anyone who comes to him must believe that he exists and that he rewards those who earnestly seek him." You cannot live a life of faith without understanding that God is a rewarder.

King David is described as a man after God's own heart (see 1 Sam 13:14). He is therefore someone who has understood what God is like. The bible says this about

David in 1 Samuel 17:26: "David asked the men standing near him, "What will be done for the man who kills this Philistine and removes this disgrace from Israel? Who is this uncircumcised Philistine that he should defy the armies of the living God?"". David is saying "what is my reward" for killing Goliath. He had a reward mindset.

In a similar way, John the apostle is described as the "beloved" apostle. He loved Jesus so much that he laid his head on Jesus as they were resting. Jesus trusted John with looking after his mother when he died. No one could ever deny that John was motivated by a love for Jesus. Yet in 2 John 1:8 he says "Watch out that you do not lose what we have worked for, but that you may be rewarded fully." John understood that God is a rewarder and wants to give you a full reward for your work.

It is therefore both legitimate and even biblical to expect and ask God for reward for your work in loving others, working for your church and expanding the kingdom. The reward will not be immediate and will require faith in God's goodness. In the parable, the Innkeeper had to trust that the Samaritan would return and settle his debts. In the same way we must trust that our God the rewarder is going to reward us for the work we do in His name for His church.

Conclusion

In pursuing God's purpose for our money and our life we can live with the expectation of reward. If you have never expected reward from God for your service, then I would suggest you pray the following prayer:

"Father, I never realised that you were a God who loves to reward your children. Can I please have the reward for the work done for your kingdom and for your church. I love you so much!"

Questions

Do you currently serve the Lord in your local church? If so, do you live with an expectation that God will reward you? If not, why not?

Day 7 - Contentment

Whilst giving to the kingdom of God must always be the primary purpose for our money, God does want us to embrace other principles in regard to our money. The second principle is contentment.

"I rejoiced greatly in the Lord that at last you renewed your concern for me. Indeed, you were concerned, but you had no opportunity to show it. I am not saying this because I am in need, for I have learned to be content whatever the circumstances. I know what it is to be in need, and I know what it is to have plenty. I have learned the secret of being content in any and every situation, whether well fed or hungry, whether living in plenty or in want. I can do all this through him who gives me strength." Phil 4:10-13

Paul was a man sitting in prison because of corrupt officials awaiting possible execution over false charges when he wrote these words. He was in a season of life which would cause most to fall into deep depression and ask why has God abandoned them.

Now the Paul who wrote this passage also wrote the passage in 2 Cor 9:8 (see day 1) that God is able to bless you with abundance in every situation. This passage does not contradict the truth of abundance, instead it emphasises a second critically important truth that we should learn - contentment.

We are all in a season or a track of life. You may be a student gaining education, you may have a job doing something which society considers to be a humble profession or you may be a professional person with great responsibility. You could be in jail or you could be in a palace. In every season or track of life, there is a call on your life to abundance. So for Joseph when he was in jail, abundance for him was to be in charge of all the other prisoners. Yet when his track in life changed and he became second in command to Pharoah, abundance looked very different. Whatever track in life you are in, God is calling you to both contentment and abundance.

The word *content* (4:11) comes from a Greek word that

means self-sufficient or independent. One element of contentment means being self-sufficient or in money terms living within your means. Many people live expecting that their track in life or season in life is about to change and so they live beyond their means. Part of contentment means that you make decisions as to how to live your life within your current means.

Contentment does not mean complacency. We are, as believers, to hold onto hopes and dreams and work to better our circumstances as we have opportunity. Paul tells slaves not to give undue concern to gaining their freedom (ie contentment), but if they are able to do so they should (1 Cor 7:21). For each of us in our circumstances there is nothing wrong with seeking an improvement in life, provided that we do not undermine our contentment in where we are at the moment. If you are in a job you don't like, there is nothing wrong with going back to school to train for a better job or from making a change to another job, as long as to do so in submission to the will of God.

Contentment is also not putting up with abuse from others. You were created as a son or daughter and King of all Kings and he did not create you to be abused.

Contentment is an inner sense of rest or peace that comes from being right with God and knowing that He is in control of all that happens to us. It means having our focus on the kingdom of God and serving Him in the track of life you are currently in. You can always pursue your money purpose with little or much.

Contentment is saying "if nothing changes I am happy with where I am now because I am pursuing God's purpose and calling on my life in my current circumstances".

Hebrews 13:5 reads "*keep your lives free from the love of money and be content with what you have, because God has said "Never will I leave you, never will I forsake you."* Contentment is the opposite of the driving force of Mammon to constantly have more money or things to give us status. Contentment is rooted in the God of all sufficiency.

Questions

Are you content where you are? Why or why not?

Are you living beyond your means because you are always looking what is going to happen next?

Prayer

"Lord, I want to live a life of contentment. I declare today that I will live within my means and reject a lifestyle of living beyond my means."

Day 8 - Excellence in Purchases

The third principle we need to understand in relation to money is excellence.

"Finally, brothers and sisters, whatever is true, whatever is noble, whatever is right, whatever is pure, whatever is lovely, whatever is admirable—if anything is excellent or praiseworthy—think about such things." Phil 4:8

In Philippians 4:8 Paul calls us to think only on pure, lovely, admirable, excellent or praiseworthy things. Why? Because what we feed our minds will determine how we live our lives. If we think about lovely, admirable, excellent things, the fruit of our lives will be lovely, admirable and excellent. Proverbs 23:7 makes this clear *"For as he thinks in his heart, so he is"*.

So the call on our lives is to think about excellent things so that our lives will reflect the excellence of our God. Further, we are to think on lovely or admirable things so our lives will reflect the beauty and creativity of our God. God is in the business of creating excellent, beautiful and wonderful things. We only have to look at what we could consider to be common flowers to realise the immense beauty and excellence in their creation.

Now God gives us money to give away and money to spend on ourselves. In 2 Cor 9:10, Paul writes: *"Now he who supplies seed to the sower and bread for food will also supply and increase your store of seed and will enlarge the harvest of your righteousness"*. Bread represents the money we have to spend on ourselves. Seed represents what we give away to others. It is important that we understand the difference between the two. Many people eat their seed by spending money on themselves, instead of giving it away as God intended. Some others are so generous that they sow their bread by giving it away. You have to realise that sowing bread only ends up in mouldy bread! God in His wisdom gives us money for giving and money to spend on ourselves.

Many believers live their lives as if God has no interest in how they spend their money or what they do with their possessions once they have purchased them. However, the God who counts the hairs on your head (Lk 12:7) is deeply interested both of these aspects of your life.

Firstly, God wants you to buy excellent or beautiful things. God wants us to think on excellent things so that our lives reflect that excellence in every ares - including what we spend we spend our money on.

As discussed in yesterday's lesson, we are all in a season or a track of life and our incomes are therefore different. So buying excellent things does not mean we all buy Ferraris to drive. It means carefully considering your purchases and buying the best you are able to do in order to represent the excellence and beauty of God. Many times it is a question of simply buying something of quality as opposed to something that will be thrown away after one use. When non-believers see what you spend your money on, are they amazed by the wisdom of your choices? They should be!

Jesus demonstrated this excellence in his material possessions. In John 19:23 we read "*When the soldiers crucified Jesus, they took his clothes, dividing them into four shares, one for each of them, with the undergarment remaining. **This garment was seamless, woven in one piece from top to bottom.**" The reason the soldiers did not divide the undergarment was because it was seamless. A seamless tunic required skill and craftsmanship beyond the norm. It was most likely an item of considerable value and thus the soldiers cast lots for it, instead of dividing it. Jesus reflected the excellence of God the Father in his material possessions.

When the Queen of Sheba met Solomon, she was overwhelmed by the following: "*all the wisdom of Solomon and the palace he had built, the food on his table, the seating of his officials, the attending servants in their robes, his cupbearers, and the burnt offerings he made at the temple of the Lord…." (1 Kings 10).* Whilst we would have all been overwhelmed by Solomon's temple (which cost hundreds of millions of dollars to build), some other aspects caught her eye as well; "*the attending servants in their robes" and "*his cupbearers*". The queen was overwhelmed by the appearance and excellence of King Solomon's servants. King Solomon promoted excellence and creativity in all areas of his life, even down to the way in which his servants were dressed and performed.

The call on our life is the same. We are to reflect the excellence, beauty and creativity of God in every aspect of our life - including the way in which we spend our money.

Yet God is not only interested in how we spend our money but also how we look after our possessions. In Proverbs 27:23-27 we read "*Be sure you know the condition of your flocks, give careful attention to your herds; for riches do not endure forever, and a crown is not secure for all generations. When the hay is removed and new growth appears and the grass from the hills is gathered in, the lambs will provide you with clothing, and the goats with the price of a field. You will have plenty of goats' milk to feed your family and to nourish your female servants.*" This passage is making it clear that we should carefully look after our material possessions because "riches do not endure forever". In other words we should not live as if we will always have more money to buy new things. Instead we should care for what we have.

This is even more important when we realise that our possessions are not ours! We are merely stewarding them for God. If He asks us to give away our possessions, we need to ensure that they are in the best condition they can be so as to bless others.

Caring for our possessions will not only increase their life cycle but demonstrates a gratefulness and thankfulness to God for His provision. If I give my daughter a new toy and she throws it on the floor at bed time so that it could be stood on, what does this say to me? It says to me that she doesn't care about what I have brought her. This is exactly the same with the provision our God gives to us.

Here are some specific examples of the stewardship of possessions:

1.   keeping your home clean and free from clutter;
2.   keeping up on small and large home repairs;

3. taking care of your furniture;
4. keeping your lawn watered and cut;
5. looking after your clothes (hanging them up at night);
6. regularly servicing your car and being careful where you park it; and
7. cleaning you car.

The test is this - if someone comes to your house, will they see the excellence and creativity of God in what you have purchased and how you have looked after it?

Questions

Do you buy things which are excellent? If not, why not?

Do you carefully look after what God has given you? If not, why not?

Prayer

"Father, I want my life to reflect your excellence. Please help me to make wise purchases and carefully look after all you have given me."

Day 9 - Multiplication

The fourth principle we need to understand and implement in our lives in relation to money is the requirement for multiplication. The following parable reflects this principle:

"Again, it will be like a man going on a journey, who called his servants and entrusted his wealth to them. To one he gave five bags of gold, to another two bags, and to another one bag, each according to his ability. Then he went on his journey. The man who had received five bags of gold went at once and put his money to work and gained five bags more. So also, the one with two bags of gold gained two more. But the man who had received one bag went off, dug a hole in the ground and hid his master's money. "After a long time the master of those servants returned and settled accounts with them. The man who had received five bags of gold brought the other five. 'Master,' he said, 'you entrusted me with five bags of gold. See, I have gained five more.' "His master replied, 'Well done, good and faithful servant! You have been faithful with a few things; I will put you in charge of many things. Come and share your master's happiness!' "The man with two bags of gold also came. 'Master,' he said, 'you entrusted me with two bags of gold; see, I have gained two more.' "His master replied, 'Well done, good and faithful servant! You have been faithful with a few things; I will put you in charge of many things. Come and share your master's happiness!' "Then the man who had received one bag of gold came. 'Master,' he said, 'I knew that you are a hard man, harvesting where you have not sown and gathering where you have not scattered seed. So I was afraid and went out and hid your gold in the ground. See, here is what belongs to you. "His master replied, 'You wicked, lazy servant! So you knew that I harvest where I have not sown and gather where I have not scattered seed? Well then, you should have put my money on deposit with the bankers, so that when I returned I would have received it back with interest."'So take the bag of gold from him and give it to the one who has ten bags. For whoever has will be given more, and they will have an abundance. Whoever does not have, even what they have will be taken from them. And throw that worthless servant outside, into the darkness, where there will be weeping and gnashing of teeth.'" Matthew 25:14-30

The moral of this parable is clear, we are to use what God has given us for increase.

It is a principle of the kingdom of God that everything we receive is to be stewarded for increase. When the sower sows the seed of the word, it is expected that there will be a harvest of multiple times what was sown (see Matthew 13). When Jesus calls us to make disciples of all nations, he intends us to take our faith and spread it to others (see Matt 28:19). It is no different in the area of money. We are to steward it for increase.

Deuteronomy 8:18 reads *"But remember the Lord your God, for it is he who gives you the ability to produce wealth, and so confirms his covenant, which he swore to your ancestors, as it is today"*. Each of us have the ability or the power to produce wealth. I have worked with many people who cannot imagine what it is to produce wealth. Yet this is what the Bible is saying. You have a choice, whether to believe your circumstances or the word of God. For those, who choose to believe His word, they will find themselves fulfilling this verse.

However, the generation of wealth is not automatic. Proverbs 21:5 provides that *"The plans of the diligent lead to profit as surely as haste leads to poverty."* Multiplication will not simply happen it requires planning and purpose.

For a lot of you, the idea of investments and multiplication of income is a million miles away. I understand that and we will explore how you can set aside money for investment over the following days. However, for the moment, I want you to grasp a principle - God wants you to increase the money he gives you so that you reflect His kingdom.

Prayer

"Father, I want to reflect your kingdom in every area of my life. Please teach me the principles for increase"

Day 10 - Prosperity of Soul (Part 1)

The pursuit of purpose in the area of money can be undermined by the enemy. Over the next two days we are going to explore how the Devil seeks to destroy abundance in your life and how you can beat his schemes.

In 3 John 1:2, the apostle John makes this important statement: "I *pray that you will prosper and be in good health as your soul prospers*"

This verse in 3 John 1:2 makes it clear that your prosperity is linked to the state of your soul. Prosperity starts with what is going on inside you. When your soul prospers, you will prosper in your finances and be in good health.

What is prosperity? When you hear the word "prosperity", how do you think it will happen in your life? Do you think of a large gift from a long lost relative? Finding a diamond on the road? Money miraculously appearing in your bank account?

Prosperity must be contrasted with provision. Prosperity is a state of living where you always have more than enough. Prosperity comes from a series of wise life decisions in the area of money and other areas of your life. Provision on the other hand is a moment in time when God gives you supernatural provision. As believers we need both provision and prosperity.

The distinction between provision and prosperity can be shown as follows. Let us say you need provision from God to meet a bill for £250. Miraculously you receive £1,000. You are very excited and give thanks to God for his radical generosity. You pay your bill and then set about shopping for new clothes and a couple of meals out. In the course of a week the £1,000 is gone. Next week your washing machine dies on you. You then buy a new washing machine for £500 and borrow money to do so. The rate of interest on your loan is 20% per year and you arrange repayments over 2 years. In this scenario, you have received divine provision yet you are not living in the state of prosperity as you are in a worse position than before your provision.

Taking the same example, let us consider how to live in prosperity. You have a bill of £250. The Lord provides you with £1,000. You thank the Lord and pay your bill. You take £500 and put into savings. You take £250 and invest it in a long term investment as you had no need for that money at the moment. That investment gives you 5% per year. Your washing machine dies and you are able to use your savings to pay for the washing machine. You receive £25 in interest over the period of 2 years on your investment which is then reinvested. In this scenario, you have received divine provision yet at the same time you are living in prosperity. You have more than enough for every season.

Prosperity flows from making long term wise decisions that are both biblical and designed to cause you to increase.

The Prospering Soul

Your soul is: (i) your mind (the way you think); (ii) your will (what you want to do and what you pursue in life); and (iii) your emotions. So our soul prospers when:

1.   you know your purpose and have a clear vision for your life;

2.   your thinking is clear and untroubled - you know how to make sensible decisions which will benefit your life;

3.   you are healthy emotionally - you are not up and down with every change of circumstance.

So what does a prosperous soul look like?

1.   you know what God has called you to and are doing it (at least in part);

2.   you believe (so it hits your emotions) the truth about yourself in every area of your life. You honestly have God's perspective on your life. There is no shame as you realise that Jesus died on the cross to take your shame and punishment; and

3.   painful losses are now hope filled and consumed in the promises of God.

What then does a non-prosperous soul look like?

1. you have inability to make logical and sensible choices because of confused and muddled thinking;

2. you make emotional choices because of how you feel;

3. you believe and live with lies about your identity and purpose; and

4. you don't have a clear purpose for your life so you make decisions which are designed to make you happy now without any reference to your future.

Example of Health

Let's apply these principles to the area of health. We are told and most people know that:

• Some exercise is good for your health

• A healthy diet containing at least 5 portions of fruit and vegetables is good for you

• An excess of sugar, fat, salt etc. is bad

The obvious question is why don't we do this then? Different people have different reasons, although there are commonly 3 main reasons.

Firstly we have confused thinking. We often hear people saying: "I'm only 40, I don't need to think about healthy eating yet", "eating healthily is too expensive....". If we scientifically analysed these statements, they would no doubt be completely untrue. However, our thinking is often confused and lacks clarity.

Secondly, our emotions decide what we eat. We refer to this as comfort eating. If you have had a terrible day, you will tend to look to chocolate or alcohol in order make yourself feel better. Certainly the last thing you feel like is exercising! This is letting our emotions make our decisions for us.

Thirdly, if we do not know what purpose God has for our life, we make decisions which feel right now without any reference to our future purpose and the plans of God for our life. If you knew that God had plans for you to reach millions of souls at the age of 85, wouldn't you think twice about abusing your body now?

As you can see, a non-prosperous soul causes you to make poor decisions on a daily basis which negatively affects your health. The same applies in the area of finances.

Application to Finances

The principles which I shall share with you in the following days have the power to set you free from debt and allow you to pursue your financial purpose in God. Yet when I have shared these principles with others, there are some that get it and put it into practice and those that understand it but do not put it into practice.

I remember clearly counselling two people both who had significant debt issues. In both cases, I was able to put together a plan for the repayment of their debt whilst maintaining their current lifestyle. One of them (Person A) ran with it and eliminated most of their debt within a very short period of time, the other (Person B) never really got started and continued living the way they had always lived.

I couldn't quite understand it - if you had the ability to continue to do what you wanted and eliminate your debt, why would you not do it? I began to consider this question in more depth.

Person A had a clear plan for their life. Whilst not a Christian, they had a clear vision for buying a house, preparing for a new child and wanted freedom in their finances. They immediately saw the benefits of adopting my proposed plan. In short their soul was relatively healthy (it had purpose and clear decision making).

Person B saw the benefits of the plan and was initially keen to pursue it. Yet at that time Person B had no clear vision or purpose for their life. Further, they would always be asking the question about what am I giving up by repaying this debt? The temptation to buy on credit cards was too great after a long hard day at work. Whilst objectively they understood the benefits of the plan, they were unable to keep to it. In short their soul was not prospering (no purpose, cluttered thinking and emotional decision making).

Poverty Spirit

If you hang around churches for a while, you are likely to hear reference to a spirit of poverty. Now the Bible does not specifically identify a demon of poverty. To a certain extent, if it did it would be easy - we know that the remedy for demonic oppression is deliverance. However, there is clearly a well orchestrated demonic attack on people's souls, the effect of which is to cause their souls to remain impoverished (and as such rob them of their prosperity). For ease of reference, I shall refer to this as a "poverty spirit".

The poverty spirit says there is never enough .... because I don't deserve it. It is an attack on your identity and purpose designed to prevent you from prospering in every area of your life. The signs of a poverty spirit are:

1. It creates anxiety and fear in the area of finances; you worry about big expenses such as your car breaking down;
2. It hoards token things mistaking clutter for wealth;
3. It believe things just happen to you and as such you avoid dreaming and making plans;
4. You want instant gratification. You make impulse purchases but resist a plan to invest or buy quality items;
5. You feel chased by troubles;
6. You feel trapped by your finances;
7. You feel overlooked and ignored it is as if your opinion is irrelevant;
8. It chokes generosity - want to give but don't feel able to do so; and
9. Tries to keep you in the same condition and you try and make sure others stay there.

Question

Do you associate with any of the signs of a poverty spirit? If so which ones?

Prayer

"Father, I pray for a soul that prospers."

Day 11 - Prosperity of Soul (Part 2)

"I pray that you will prosper and be in good health as your soul prospers"
3 John 1:2

Yesterday we looked at what a prosperous soul looked like and why it was important. We also considered the impact of the spirit of poverty on a person's soul and the decisions they make in life. Today we are going to look at breaking the power of the spirit of poverty over your life.

Poverty is an organised attack on a persons belief system Proverbs 23:7 reads *"As a man thinks within himself so he is"*. By attacking your belief system about yourself, the devil is seeking to change the way you think about yourself. He wants you to think you are worthless and powerless in all areas of your life. The reason he wants to do this is because if he can get you to think that, you **will become** worthless and powerless. As you think you are. Thus poverty is like a radio or television station which constantly broadcasts lies about who you are.

Mark 4:24 reads *""Consider carefully what you hear," he continued. "With the measure you use, it will be measured to you—and even more."* When Jesus says "consider carefully what you hear" he is not suggesting we walk around with ear plugs in, in order to avoid hearing anything. What he is talking about is be careful what you listen to or more precisely what you give attention to. Whatever we listen to will gain our focus and attention and without knowing it will begin to shape our beliefs and values. These beliefs and values then set a standard for which voices we pick out of our environment. So we effectively filter out those messages which are contrary to what we believe and feed even more on the messages that we initially gave our attention to.

By means of example, if you turn your attention to say a particular political party's views (let's call these the Party A) those views will shape your beliefs and values. You will begin to believe those values and they will define how you see yourself. When alternative political views are expressed (say Party B views), you will measure them against what you have been listening to and reject them. Yet when you hear more of Party A's views, you will accept them as they agree with what you believe. Thus you will surround yourself with views which agree with what you believe.

Why do gossips always attract other gossips? The reason being is that person has given their ear to gossip and they will continue to feed themselves on gossip.

This is particularly important in relation to the poverty spirit. The poverty spirit is constantly broadcasting how worthless and powerless you are. If you listen to it it will define how you think about yourself. You will then look for more messages which confirm how worthless and powerless you are. Believe me there are plenty of demons willing to give you that message!

Yet let us consider what happens if you listen to what God says about you. He says you are valuable and have been brought at the ultimate price (Romans 5:8 "*But God demonstrates His own love toward us, in that while we were still sinners, Christ died for us")*. He says you are powerful (Ephesians 3:17-20 "*I pray that out of his glorious riches he may **strengthen you with power** through his Spirit in your inner being, so that Christ may dwell in your hearts through faith. ..…... Now to him who is able to do immeasurably more than all we ask or imagine, **according to his power that is at work within us**, to him be glory in the church and in Christ Jesus throughout all generations, for ever and ever! Amen.".* If you are listening to what God says about you - guess what, you will end up living as both valuable and powerful! What is more, when you turn your attention to what God has to say about you, you will filter out what the devil wants to say about you and you will keep hearing more and more about how much God thinks about you.

As you feed yourselves on what God says about you, your soul will prosper and you will begin to see a transformation.

1.   Where poverty creates constant worry, the prosperous soul is anxious for   nothing. You know that God is faithful and you live with a deep understanding of that faithfulness.

2.   Where poverty hoards, prosperity conserves and uses. You find creative and beneficial ways to look after and recycle your possessions.

3.   Where poverty believes that things just happen to me, the prosperous soul believes 'I'm here to be a blessing'. You dream of how to use your gifts to make the world better.

4.   Where poverty reaches for instant gratification, a prosperous soul exercises self control in working towards goals and priorities. You take time to budget for important things.

5.   Where a poverty spirit hounds you, a prosperous soul brings contentment. As you pursue your destiny you do so from a place of rest and gratitude.

6.   Whilst a poverty spirit feels out of control, a prosperous soul protects and delights in the unlimited access to the strength and wisdom of God. Even in the place of mistakes you know you can seek Him in order to both rescue you and teach you

7.   Where the poverty spirit hides you, the prosperous soul is entirely secure knowing you have the attention and favour of God.

8.   Where the poverty spirit chokes generosity, the prosperous soul delights in it. You love to give.

9.   Where the poverty spirit seeks to keep you and others in the same place, the prosperous soul seeks continual expansion and growth and seeks to empower others.

For those of you reading this who recognise that they are suffering from a poverty spirit, it is time to deal with it! I have found that a poverty spirit causes people to hide from their finances and never get started with the process of sorting them out. This shame needs to be broken by the power of the Holy Spirit.

To start with, we need to invite God to speak to us:

Prayers

"Father God, I am your child. Thank you for your goodness and faithfulness. I need your grace to discover the lies I have trusted, and ask You show them to me"

For each of you, the devil has been attacking your identity by telling you lies. It is now time for those lies to be identified. The lies you have believed will be personal to you, but some examples of common lies are set out below:

Lies of fear - I'm afraid of failure/success things are going too well; I am too much trouble; I can't succeed because of past mistakes

Lies of shame and worthlessness - what I think doesn't matter' I am worthless; I'm just a ....; I am too stupid; my family is cursed' I don't deserve money or health; I've made too many mistakes

Lies of hopelessness - problems in my life won't change; I'm destined to be poor; I'm too young/old' I can never escape my debt

Lies about money - the rich are unhappy; wealth - evil; money controls you; it's too much work to make money; you have to have money to make money.

Spend some time listening to God. He will show you which lies you have been listening to.

Once you have heard from God, it is time to start dealing with these lies. Father God I recognise that these lies create destructive forces in my life. I recognise that You did not teach me these things, but I have learned them from people and events in my past.

Prayers

I forgive these people now. I forgive _____ and release him/her into Your hand"

"I forsake those events now. I forgive myself for _____ and release them into Your hand"

I ask you, Father, to strike these lies at the root and sever their effect in my life, my family's history and my family's future.

Finally, Father, I ask You to replace each of these lies with biblical truth. Occupy my heart with Your work. Improve my soil and bless my destiny as a prosperous soul. Bless my family tree with abundant life.

I would recommend that you then take two pieces of paper. One with the lie on it and one with the truth on it. Destroy the one with the lie on it and as you destroy it, at the same time pray: "I sever by faith in Jesus Christ, the root lie of _____ right now"

More Information

For more on this issue of the Poverty Spirit and how to deal with it, I would strongly recommend the book "Money and the Prosperous Soul" by Stephen De Silva. Some of the lists set out above and prayers at the end of this book are taken from his work.

SECTION 2 - WISDOM

Day 12 - Faith and Wisdom

" When Jesus heard what had happened, he withdrew by boat privately to a solitary place. Hearing of this, the crowds followed him on foot from the towns. When Jesus landed and saw a large crowd, he had compassion on them and healed their sick.
As evening approached, the disciples came to him and said, "This is a remote place, and it's already getting late. Send the crowds away, so they can go to the villages and buy themselves some food." Jesus replied, "They do not need to go away. You give them something to eat."
"We have here only five loaves of bread and two fish," they answered.
"Bring them here to me," he said. And he directed the people to sit down on the grass. Taking the five loaves and the two fish and looking up to heaven, he gave thanks and broke the loaves. Then he gave them to the disciples, and the disciples gave them to the people. They all ate and were satisfied, and the disciples picked up twelve basketfuls of broken pieces that were left over. The number of those who ate was about five thousand men, besides women and children." Matt 14:13-21

This passage demonstrates Jesus' approach to provision. When we read the passage we are immediately drawn to the extravagant and amazing miracle of turning 5 loaves and 2 fishes into food for 5,000 men (which does not include the women and children who were also there). This was a miracle of faith. Jesus exercised radical faith for supernatural increase.

Yet it is easy to miss the second part of this event. Once everyone had been fed, he told his disciples to pick up the broken pieces that were left over. Why did Jesus do this? Because he realised that he was accountable for everything that God had provided for him. He could not be complacent or negligent with any part of God's provision. It was all precious and all had a purpose. This is wisdom being demonstrated.

As believers, we are required to walk in faith **and** wisdom for our finances. Faith without wisdom will result in the blessings of the Lord being lost or squandered. Wisdom without faith will limit your blessings to that which you can humanly manage. Further, the exercise of wisdom outside of the context of faith tends towards self sufficiency - this is fatal for believers.

The Basis of Our Faith

Wealth was created by God for man. In Haggai 2:8 we read "*the silver is mine and the gold is mine declares the Lord Almighty*". God is therefore is the owner of our wealth. Yet we read in Genesis 2:12 in relation to the Garden of Eden, "*The gold of that land is good.*" In Genesis 2:15, Adam was to work and take care of the garden. He was put in charge of it. Thus Adam was put in charge of gold and silver resources.

Yet when Adam sinned, he gave away the rights to the resources and riches of this world. We can see this clearly in the temptation of Jesus in Luke 4: 5-7: "*The devil led him up to a high place and showed him in an instant all the kingdoms of the world. And he said to him, "I will give you all their authority and splendor; it has been given to me, and I can give it to anyone I want to. If you worship me, it will all be yours.*" Note that the devil says that the splendour or the riches of the kingdoms of the world belong to the devil because "it has been given to me". Who gave him the riches? Adam did when he sinned. Note that Jesus does not correct the devil's understanding by saying "you don't own them". Instead Jesus emphasises the requirement to serve and worship the owner of the wealth (God) as opposed to its steward (the devil).

Yet through the death and resurrection of Jesus he has reclaimed the wealth of the world for his people. In Revelation 5:12 we read the following about Jesus: "*Worthy is the Lamb, who was slain, to receive power and **wealth** and wisdom and strength and honour and glory and praise*". Jesus now has the legal right to the wealth of the world. Further he shares that right with believers. In Eph 2:6 we read "*And God raised us up with Christ and seated us with him in the heavenly realms in Christ Jesus*". So Jesus has the right to all wealth and we are seated with Christ in Christ. So whatever belongs to Jesus also belongs to us as believers (as we are in Christ). We have a legal right to the wealth that belongs to Jesus.

However, the devil is described as a thief. He is happy to hold onto wealth which belongs to you. He is happy to steal from you wealth that you have a legal right to. How do we exercise our legal rights? In short, through faith. We will explore in Section 3 how to exercise faith for increase.

Wisdom

What is wisdom? In Proverbs 3:19 we read: "*By wisdom the Lord laid the earth's foundations*".   Wisdom is described in this verse as the architect which has planned and mapped out the way in which the earth works. Thus to walk in wisdom is to walk in the way in which God intended us to walk.

As we walk in wisdom, we tap into the way in which God designed us to live. We should therefore not be surprised that as we walk in wisdom we will see blessings abound in our life, simply because we are operating in the way which we were created to operate. King Solomon probably the wisest man on earth (before Jesus) demonstrated wisdom in all areas of life including finances. We read in 1 Kings 10:27 the effect of a kingdom ruled by wisdom: "*The king made silver as common in Jerusalem as stones, and cedar as plentiful as sycamore-fig trees in the foothills.*" We should not be surprised that as we pursue wisdom we see an increase in wealth and finances.

Over the following days we will explore the role of wisdom in our finances.

Questions

Did you realise that you had a legal right to wealth? How does that change the way you view your financial position?

Do you treat every penny that God gives you as important? If not, why not?

Prayer

"Father, I want a teachable spirit. Help me to learn and apply the lessons in the area of faith and wisdom for finances. Lord I pray for both wisdom and an increase in faith".

Day 13 - Wisdom Overview

"By wisdom a house is built, and through understanding it is established" Proverbs 24:3

In order to establish a prosperous household, you need wisdom. Wisdom both preserves and enriches every aspect of your life. The book of Proverbs identifies seven foundational principles in the area of finances. These are:

1.   The Tithe

Proverbs 3:9 provides that you should: "*Honor the Lord with your wealth, with the firstfruits of all your crops; then your barns will be filled to overflowing, and your vats will brim over with new wine*". It is God's plan that you establish the tithe in your life so that your life will be blessed.

2.   Offerings

Proverbs 11:25 reads that "*A generous person will prosper; whoever refreshes others will be refreshed.*" Wisdom dictates that generosity will be rewarded. Proverbs 19:17 specifically addresses being generous to the poor "*Whoever is kind to the poor lends to the Lord, and he will reward them for what they have done.*" Generosity is a key to financial increase.

3.   Savings

Proverbs 13:11 says: "*Dishonest money dwindles away, but whoever gathers money little by little makes it grow.*" Saving is a principle of wisdom. By gathering small amounts of money on regular occasions, you can quickly save significant sums of money.

4.   Investment

Proverbs 21:5 reads "*The plans of the diligent lead to profit*". It is wisdom to develop sound investment plans and these will lead to profit. In Ecc 11:2 it reads: "*Invest in seven ventures, yes, in eight; you do not know what disaster may come upon the land."* There is wisdom in diversification of investments.

5. **Being Debt Free**

Proverbs 3:27 states: *"Do not withhold good from those to whom it is due, when it is in your power to act."* The starting point is that we must repay our debts and make repayment of debts a priority in our lives. Proverbs 22:7 establishes an important principle *"The rich rule over the poor, and the borrower is slave to the lender."* Every time we borrow money our freedom is compromised, we are enslaved to our lender. No longer are we free to make free choices in relation to our money and career because we have to ensure that we repay the debt. In Proverbs 17:18 we read: *"One who has no sense shakes hands in pledge and puts up security for a neighbour."* Wisdom dictates that giving guarantees for others when you have no control over those people's actions is foolish.

6. **Strong Work Ethic**

Proverbs 14:23 provides that *"All hard work brings a profit but mere talk leads only to poverty."* It is wise to work hard. It will lead you into profit. Proverbs 10:4 reinforces this principle when it says:*"Lazy hands make for poverty, but diligent hands bring wealth."* For those who enjoy their sleeping, there are some sobering words in Proverbs 6:10 *"A little sleep, a little slumber, a little folding of the hands to rest—and poverty will come on you like a thief and scarcity like an armed man."* A strong work ethic is wisdom.

7. **Budgeting and Financial Planning**

Proverbs 21:20 reads: *"The wise store up choice food and olive oil, but fools gulp theirs down."* The principle is clear, when you receive money or goods, it is wisdom to plan how you spend or consume them. Spending all of your money when you get it is foolishness. This requires putting in place a budget for your finances. Proverbs 24:27 reads: *"Put your outdoor work in order and get your fields ready; after that, build your house."* This verse addresses the priority of how we spend our money and time. It is wisdom to prioritise our investments and sources of income (i.e. the outdoor work) before concentrating on our own comfort. Proverbs 13:22 reads: "*A good person leaves an inheritance for their children's children*". Long term planning to bless generations is expected of believers.

We will explore these principles of wisdom in more detail over the coming days.

Question

Do you have a financial plan in your life which includes each of these principles of wisdom? If not, which elements of wisdom are you currently not pursuing?

Which of these principles do you find the most difficult to accept? Why?

Prayer

"Father I want to align my finances with your principles of wisdom. Please give me grace to understand and establish wisdom in the area of my finances"

Day 14 - Budgeting (Part 1)

The first practical step you must take in relation to your finances is understanding what you earn (your income) and what you spend (your expenditure). Most people know what they earn but have little concept of what they are spending.

STAGE 1

In order to start this exercise, you will need to gather information from your last 3 month's of spending (bank statements, receipts etc). When you fill out the form (found at Appendix 1), make sure you take the average of the last 3 months' spending. So for example, if you spent £20 on clothes in January, £30 in February and £100 in March, the average monthly spend would be £50.

The form of the Current Monthly Budget is set out in Appendix 1. Fill it in - it will take you a while to do this but, do take the time and effort to do this properly.

Once you have completed this process, you will find that either:

1.   You have more income than expenditure;
2.   Your income and expenditure are the same; or
3.   Your expenditure is greater than your income.

STAGE 2

Whichever category you are in, the next stage will be the same: you are to find savings. In the same way as Jesus gathered the scraps after feeding the 5000, you are to look for savings on your expenses. These savings are really important in helping you with your financial future.

Savings fall into three broad categories:

1.   Checking that you receive all the correct income you are entitled to/are paying the right amount of tax

Depending on which country you live in, you may well be entitled to benefits from the government. You need to make sure you are receiving all of the benefits you are entitled to. You may well find that there are helpful websites that can you help with working this out (e.g. Moneysavingexpert in the UK). Certain voluntary organisations may also be able to help (such as the Citizens Advice Bureau in the UK).

Further, make sure you are paying the right amount of tax and claiming any tax benefits you could be entitled to. An example of this would be that if you are a higher rate tax payer in the UK, you are entitled to money back on your charitable donations including those you give to the Church.

Take time to work through these questions as they can be the difference between hundreds of pounds (or whatever currency you are working in!) of income per month.

2.   Check Your Expenses and Look For Savings

It has been my experience that many people are overpaying for their basic services such as gas, electric, insurance on their car or house, mobile phone costs etc. Take time to go through each of your expenses and see if you can save money on each item. There are a number of price comparison websites which can help you with this process.

We also often overpay for our groceries. We often don't realise that supermarkets are carefully designed to get you to spend more than you would ordinarily spend. I would strongly recommend that as a household you draw up meal plans for the week (rather than leaving it to the last minute). Then make a shopping list in order to purchase the items you need (and stick to that list!).

There are many online resources that can help you identify savings and ways of doing day to day tasks which will save you money. Take time to go through these. This will take several days of time and effort. Set time aside to do this.

3.   Sell Your Unwanted Possessions

We can often accumulate a lot of stuff. I would go around your house and ask yourself the question "will I use this item in the next 12 months". Be strict with yourself. If the answer is "no" then you should think about selling it. You would be amazed how much people would pay for your unwanted items.

This process is particularly important if a large amount of your monthly expenditure is used to pay debts. You should be using the cash generated from these sales to pay down your loans and reducing your debts.

Prayer

"Father give me grace and the strength to get to grip with my finances. Help me in the areas I find difficult. Remove all shame of finances because I am coming to you and presenting them before you, knowing you will redeem every part of my life."

Day 15 - Budgeting (Part 2)

"Blessed are the meek, for they will inherit the earth." Matt 5:5

We often think of meekness as powerlessness. When we consider that Jesus (who was the all powerful God come to earth in human form) was said to be meek (2 Cor 10:1), we soon realise it cannot mean powerlessness.

Jesus was described as meek because He voluntarily limited Himself to use only a small percentage of available power. Meekness is choosing to limit the use of available resources or power. A meek person is one who has great power or resources, but voluntarily limits themselves to use only a percentage of that resource or power.

Meekness has a role to play in our finances. Meekness is displayed when we choose to live within a percentage of our income (as opposed to spending it all). The voluntary limiting ourselves (or living below our means) positions us for greater things (inheriting the earth).

With this in mind, we turn to the third stage of our budgeting process. Setting limits on our expenditure.

STAGE 3 - LIMITS

Once you have completed the exercise of recording your income and expenditure and have found savings, the next step is to set limits on how much you are going to allow yourself to spend.

My grandma had very little money but was incredibly careful with what she did have. When she received her housekeeping money each week she would separate her money and put different amounts into envelopes. One envelope was for the grocers shop and this was filled with a certain amount of money, another envelope was for the milk man who would deliver the milk - money was set aside in this envelope to cover those costs, one was for the fish seller, one was for insurance etc. By doing this exercise she was separating money for a purpose and at the same time setting a limit to the amount of money she would spend on each item. This method of budgeting is effective and is often referred to as the envelope system.

However, many of us do not hold our money in cash form, so we can put it into envelopes. Most of us have money in a bank account. Yet it is really important to create virtual envelopes for your spending. These virtual envelopes perform the same job as the actual envelope used by my grandma: (i) they set aside money for purpose; and (ii) they set a limit on your spending in that area.

For example, you may find that you are spending too much on clothes, technology, eating out etc. now is the time to set a set a sensible limit on how much you can spend each month. Go through this process with God. Let Him show you how much you should be spending.

Once you have completed this process, you will have decided how much you should be spending in each category of your life.

The types of categories you would set limits for are:

1.   food;
2.   clothes;
3.   eating out/socialising; and
4.   general spending etc.

You will want to set a limit for every category that you have a discretion as to how much to spend.

You now need a method of keeping to this limit or budget. If you have your money in cash, then use the envelope system. For those whose money is in a bank account and if you have a smartphone consider using one of the many budget applications available (most of which are free of charge). These will allow you to set your budget and record every expenditure you make. If you do not have a smartphone or don't like using them, make sure you keep a paper record of what you spending in each area.

The most important things to ensure you do is: (i) stick to your budgets; and (ii) make sure you have a method of recording every expenditure and keeping track of how much you have left to spend. Small expenditure is often missed but adds up to large amounts of money.

STAGE 4 - THE ASSESSMENT

Once you have found savings and set limits to your spending, you will be in one of three categories:

1.   Have money to spare;
2.   Have broken even; or
3.   Are still spending more than you earn.

If you fall into category 1, then you have made a start towards living in meekness. If you fall in category 3 (or possibly 2), then it is fair to say that this position will not sustainable over a long period of time. So you need to identify the cause of the over-spending. The most likely causes are:

1.   **Problems with income** - you may have lost your job, you may be forced to work in work that isn't paying anywhere near enough to sustain your family. You may be having problems with state benefits.

2.   **Problems with debt** - for many people the cost of their debt is crippling, the monthly cost of debt has meant that they cannot afford their other household expenses.

3.   **Special costs** - for some people they have special costs they cannot avoid, such as the costs of caring for a loved one.

For a number of people, the problems can be a mixture of 1, 2 or 3. If debt forms part of your problems, then the starting point is to find a lump sum to pay down some of your most expensive debt (although do check the position on early repayment costs). This lump sum is either found by using some of your savings (if you have any) or selling any goods that are non-essential.   Payment of the highest interest debts will free more money up each month. See if this helps to bring your expenditure below your income.

If after considering the position with God you are honestly unable to find a lump sum, then you are the perfect candidate for a miracle! If God has given us the resources to meet our debts then we should exhaust those first, but once we have done that, we can expect our Father to intervene and provide supernaturally. In order to access this provision, we will need to exercise faith (see Section 3).

For those with low incomes or special costs, you are going to need to walk in faith for an increase in income or a lowering of costs.

Prayer

"Father, the promise is that the meek shall inherit the earth. Give me grace and ability to walk in meekness in relation to my finances."

Day 16 - Budgeting (Part 3)

"A good person leaves an inheritance for their children's children"
Proverbs 13:22

If we accept that a good person leaves an inheritance not just for your children but for your grandchildren, how do plan to do this? Have you ever thought about how you can achieve this? This scripture is not talking about a token gift for your grandchildren but something substantive that will give them a head start in life. Will it simply happen without a plan?

The short answer for most of us is that we have not given any serious thought as to how to bless generations. Yet God is calling us to do just that! In order to do so, we need a plan.

The starting point for financial planning is the creation of "Pots". When I was teaching my daughter about this principle I made her a money box (see below). Whilst the woodworkers among you may despair, please look beyond the craftsmanship to the principle!

There are five compartments on the box:

1. the tithe;
2. offerings;
3. savings;
4. investment; and
5. spending.

She was to divide the money she received from my wife and I into the following proportions:

1. the tithe - 10%
2. offerings - 20%
3. savings - 10%
4. investment - 20%
5. spending - 40%

The tithe was paid to the local church. Offerings were to give away as she felt led. Savings were kept so she could make larger purchases. Investments were used to buy card making equipment which she would use to make cards which were sold for profit. Spending was for spending each week as she wanted.

So many people I have spoken to have no concept of keeping separate pots of money for different purposes. Yet this is exactly what you need to do. I would suggest that the percentages that I have set for my daughter is a very healthy aim as it rightly prioritises giving whilst maintaining balance amongst savings and investment. Yet for some of us, we know the call of God to give more than 30% of our income.

However, I accept for those of you who are new to this process, it is important to set realistic targets for the distribution of your pots.

Start by working out where you are with your current financial situation and then set a realistic goal for how you can allocate money between your pots. Fill out the table below by completing the following tasks:

1. Fill out how much you currently give to tithing, offering, savings, investment and spending;

2. Work out what this is as a percentage of your income (this is how you work it out: divide the amount you spend in each pot by your total income. Multiply that figure by 100. That will give you a percentage);

3. Decide how you can divide your current money between your pots. In terms of priority, I would recommend the following:

    (a) start with allocating 10% to your tithe;
    (b) next look to allocate 5% of your money into savings;
    (c) next consider investments and offerings and allocate money to those in equal proportions until you reach 20% for each.
    (d) then look to bring your income to ideal levels set out above.

Many of you may not even be able to reach (a). That's fine, we will be exploring how you can move in faith for increase in Section 3.

4. Then decide what you are going to do **when** you get more income. It is amazing how quickly we spend any increase. Yet if you have already decided how much money is enough (by setting limits) then you should not fall into the trap of simply expanding your lifestyle to meet your income. Plan in advance where your money will be allocated (say between offerings and investment).

As your income increases, you will want to revisit this table and decide again how to allocate your money. This is the start of your financial planning.

Pot	Currently - How much do I put in £'s into each pot	Currently Percentages	Target for now	Aim for you when you get more income
Tithe	£	%	%	%
Offerings	£	%	%	%
Savings	£	%	%	%
Investments	£	%	%	%
Spending	£	%	%	%

Some Tips

1. Never mix pots - keep them separate. Do not be tempted to move offerings into savings etc.

2. Keep pots physically separate - possibly different bank accounts. Make savings and investment more difficult to get hold of. This will prevent temptation to dip into them.

3. Allocate your money the moment you get paid. Do not delay or else the temptation to spend it will become greater.

Prayer

"Father, I want to leave an inheritance to my children's children. Give me a plan to bless my family for generations"

Day 17 - Tithe (Part 1 - The History of the Tithe)

"Bring all the tithes into the storehouse, that there may be food in My house, And try Me in this; says the Lord of hosts "If I will not open for you the windows of heaven, And pour out for you such blessing, That there will not be room enough to receive it" Mal 3:10

The most important priority in your financial planning is to establish your tithe. This is the starting point of fulfilling the primary purpose for your money (ie giving to the kingdom of God) and opens doors to blessings which otherwise would be closed.

What is the tithe? The tithe is a translation of a Hebrew word "masser"which simply means 10%. You cannot tithe 8% or 9% because the tithe means 10%. So to give your tithe is to give 10% of your income. Your income is your pay or other profits from investments.

Since I have been teaching about finances, the one area that leads to more discussion (or argument/debate) is the issue of the tithe. We should not find this surprising as the tithe is the entry level of giving and opens up the door to blessings in your life which would otherwise not be open. Most people who tithe quickly move onto giving offerings and truly embrace God's purpose for their money. Those who do not honour the tithe tend to struggle in many areas of their life and never get to fulfil the primary purpose for their money. I can say with confidence that the devil does not want you to tithe.

However, given the huge number of varying teachings on the tithe, I thought it worthwhile to set out in some detail the history of the tithe. In short, I will demonstrate that the tithe was established in the life of Abraham, the father of our faith, was ratified by the law and approved of by Jesus and has application today.

Established by Abraham

Abraham lived 430 years before the Jewish law. So anything that Abraham does cannot be said to be "law".

The first mention of the tithe in the bible is found in Genesis

14:18 which reads: *"Then Melchizedek king of Salem brought out bread and wine. He was priest of God Most High, and he blessed Abram, saying, "Blessed be Abram by God Most High, Creator of heaven and earth. And praise be to God Most High, who delivered your enemies into your hand." Then Abram* **gave him a tenth of everything."**

The significance of this encounter cannot be underestimated and is highlighted in Hebrews 7: *"This Melchizedek was king of Salem and priest of God Most High. He met Abraham returning from the defeat of the kings and blessed him, and Abraham gave him a tenth of everything. First, the name Melchizedek means "king of righteousness"; then also, "king of Salem" means "king of peace." Without father or mother, without genealogy, without beginning of days or end of life, resembling the Son of God, he remains a priest forever. Just think how great he was: Even the patriarch Abraham gave him a tenth of the plunder! Now the law requires the descendants of Levi who become priests to collect a tenth from the people—that is, from their fellow Israelites—even though they also are descended from Abraham. This man, however, did not trace his descent from Levi, yet he collected a tenth from Abraham and blessed him who had the promises. And without doubt the lesser is blessed by the greater. In the one case, the tenth is collected by people who die;* **but in the other case, by him who is declared to be living**. *One might even say that Levi, who collects the tenth, paid the tenth through Abraham, because when Melchizedek met Abraham, Levi was still in the body of his ancestor."*

The writer of Hebrews is making some amazing points here:

1.   **Melchizedek** - Melchizidek represents Jesus. His name means "king of righteousness" or "king of peace". He has no father or mother (as Jesus who was begotten not created) and resembles the Son of God.

2.   **Abraham** - Abraham was the father of the Jewish nation including the tribe of Levi from whom the priests were chosen. Abraham is also the father of our faith as Christians (see Romans 3).

3.   **The Tithe** - Abraham as the father of our faith gave 10% of everything he had. He gave it to a person who

clearly represents Jesus.

Thus there is a principle established in the life of Abraham that a tithe is paid to God.

Jacob

Jacob was Abraham's son. In Genesis 28:22, we see that Jacob adopts the principle of the tithe that his father demonstrated: *"Then Jacob made a vow, saying, "If God will be with me and will watch over me on this journey I am taking and will give me food to eat and clothes to wear so that I return safely to my father's household, then the Lord will be my God and this stone that I have set up as a pillar will be God's house, and of all that you give me I will give you a tenth."* Note that Jacob's tithe was also established before the law.

The Law

The law ratified the principle of the tithe and introduced it as law to the Jewish people. Yet there appear to be three separate tithes established by the law:

1.   the Levite tithe;
2.   the worship tithe; and
3.   the poor tithe.

The Levite Tithe

The Levite tithe was the basic tithe the people of Israel were to give. It was given to the Levites to support them as they had no land of their own.

In Leviticus 27:30 we read *"A tithe of everything from the land, whether grain from the soil or fruit from the trees, belongs to the Lord; it is holy to the Lord. Whoever would redeem any of their tithe must add a fifth of the value to it. Every tithe of the herd and flock—every tenth animal that passes under the shepherd's rod—will be holy to the Lord."* Note that the tithe is described as "holy". This means it is set aside for God and cannot be used for anything else.

In Numbers 21 we can read: *"I give to the Levites all the tithes in Israel as their inheritance in return for the work they do while serving at the tent of meeting. From now on the Israelites must not go near the tent of meeting, or they will bear the consequences of their sin and will die. It is the Levites who are to do the work at the tent of meeting and bear the responsibility for any offenses they commit against it. This is a lasting ordinance for the generations to come. They will receive no inheritance among the Israelites. Instead, I give to the Levites as their inheritance the tithes that the Israelites present as an offering to the Lord. That is why I said concerning them: 'They will have no inheritance among the Israelites.'"* As we can see, the primary purpose of the tithe was to support the role of the priests or Levites.

This tithe is also mentioned again in Neh 10:37 *"Moreover, we will bring to the storerooms of the house of our God, to the priests, the first of our ground meal, of our grain offerings, of the fruit of all our trees and of our new wine and olive oil. And we will bring a tithe of our crops to the Levites, for it is the Levites who collect the tithes in all the towns where we work."* As part of the rebuilding of Jerusalem it was necessary to re-establish the importance of the Levite tithe.

It is the Levite tithe which best represents the tithe paid by Abraham to Melchizidek. This is the tithe we would honour today.

The Worship Tithe

This tithe is highlighted in Deut 12:17 *"You must not eat in your own towns the tithe of your grain and new wine and olive oil, or the firstborn of your herds and flocks, or whatever you have vowed to give, or your freewill offerings or special gifts. Instead, you are to eat them in the presence of the Lord your God at the place the Lord your God will choose—you, your sons and daughters, your male and female servants, and the Levites from your towns—and you are to rejoice before the Lord your God in everything you put your hand to. Be careful not to neglect the Levites as long as you live in your land.""*

It is also mentioned in Deut 14:22 *"Be sure to set aside a tenth of all that your fields produce each year. Eat the tithe of your grain, new wine and olive oil, and the firstborn of your herds and flocks in the presence of the Lord your God at the place he will choose as a dwelling for his Name, so that you may learn to revere the Lord your God always. But if that place is too distant and you have been blessed by the Lord your God and cannot carry your tithe (because the place where the Lord will choose to put his Name is so far away), then exchange your tithe for silver, and take the silver with you and go to the place the Lord your God will choose. Use the silver to buy whatever you like: cattle, sheep, wine or other fermented drink, or anything you wish. Then you and your household shall eat there in the presence of the Lord your God and rejoice. And do not neglect the Levites living in your towns, for they have no allotment or inheritance of their own."*

The notion that this tithe was separate from the Levite tithe is found in the apocryphal book of Tobit 1:7. It appears to be a tithe which you bring to the Lord and use to celebrate or worship God with in a feast. It is linked to the Jewish celebrations.

The Poor Tithe

The poor tithe is mentioned in Deut 14:28:   *"At the end of every three years, bring all the tithes of that year's produce and store it in your towns, so that the Levites (who have no allotment or inheritance of their own) and the foreigners, the fatherless and the widows who live in your towns may come and eat and be satisfied, and so that the Lord your God may bless you in all the work of your hands."*

This tithe is only given every three years and is designed solely to look after the poor.

The Law and the Tithes

Whilst I have demonstrated that the principle of the tithe predates the law, the question is "are we required to follow the law in giving three separate tithes?" I think the short answer is no. The principle of giving 10% to God is founded before the law. The law confirms the importance of the tithe and also makes provision for additional tithes for worship and the poor.

We are not required to follow all three tithes, but we are to realise that there is God given wisdom in noting the importance that God gives to each of these areas.

Jesus and the Tithe

Whilst the tithe was founded by Abraham, the father of our faith and was ratified by the law, it was also approved by Jesus.

When the Pharisees came to challenge Jesus about the issue of paying tax, Jesus says in Mark 12:17 *""Give back to Caesar what is Caesar's and to God what is God's."* Giving to Caesar what is Caesar's is easy to understand. Jesus is saying to pay your tax. Giving to God what is God's would have been clearly understood by the Jewish people who understood "give to God what is God's" to be a reference to the tithe. Here Jesus is positively approving of the tithe.

Jesus does this again in Matt 23:23 where he says *"Woe to you, teachers of the law and Pharisees, you hypocrites! You give a tenth of your spices—mint, dill and cumin. But you have neglected the more important matters of the law— justice, mercy and faithfulness. You should have practiced the latter, without neglecting the former."* Whilst Jesus tells the Pharisees off for neglecting justice and mercy, he at the same time confirms that they should be tithing.

Conclusion

It is clear throughout scripture that the tithe is an eternal principle. In Malachi 3:6 immediately before the verses on tithing, we read *"I the Lord do not change"*. God is trying to make it clear to us as believers that the tithe is for us now. It represents God's minimum standards of giving for His people.

Questions

Do you currently tithe? If not why not? If it is for theological reasons has your view changed?

Prayer

"Father, I want to live in the fulness of what you have for me. I realise that the tithe is important to you. I thank you for the opportunity to give 10% of my income to you."

Day 18 - The Tithe (Part 2)

Which 10%

If we have established that the tithe requires us to pay 10% of what we earn to the Lord, the question is which 10%? In Proverbs 3:9 we read: "*Honor the Lord with your wealth, with the **firstfruits** of all your crops; then your barns will be filled to overflowing, and your vats will brim over with new wine.*"

God is asking us to take the firstfruits and give it to Him. We can see this principle demonstrated in the life of Cain and Abel. In Genesis 4 we read: "*Now Abel kept flocks, and Cain worked the soil. In the course of time Cain brought some of the fruits of the soil as an offering to the Lord. And Abel also brought an offering—fat portions from some of the firstborn of his flock. The Lord looked with favor on Abel and his offering, but on Cain and his offering he did not look with favor.*"

What was the difference between Cain's offering and Abel's offering? Abel brought an offering from the "firstborn" of his flock. Cain brought an offering of "some of the fruits of the soil". Abel gave the firstborn of his flocks. So when Abel gave, he did not know how many more lambs he would get. It was an act of faith to give his first. Cain on the other hand collected all his food together and then decided to give God some. His offering required no faith whereas Abel's did.

When God gave his only son, we can see in Col 1:15 that Jesus is described as the firstborn. God gave his first.

So what does this mean for us? The payment of our tithe should come before anything else is taken from our pay or income. It should come before tax, bills and other expenses. The temptation is to wait until the end of the month to see if you can afford your tithe. This is not what God intended for you. He wanted you to live by faith and give Him your first 10%.

If we give our tithe before tax, then it means that we pay our tithe on the gross sum that we earn. For example, if you earn £1,000 per month (before tax) your tithe is £100 per month.

Where do we pay our tithe?

Malachi 3:6 onwards reads: *"For I am the Lord, I do not change; ..... Will a man rob God? Yet you have robbed Me! But you say "In what way have we robbed You?" In tithes and offerings. .... Bring all the tithes into the* **storehouse***, that there may be food in my house"*.

In the Old Testament the tithe was given to the local priests who were carrying out God's work. The same is true today. We give our tithes to the local church we are attending. There can be a desire or a tendency to try and pay our tithe to whatever Christian cause takes our fancy. This is what offerings are for, not the tithe. The tithe is to be paid to the church you are attending to support the ministers in that church.

What happens if you don't pay your tithe?

Leviticus 27:30 says this *"And all the tithe of the land, whether of the seed of the land or of the first fruit of the tree, is the Lord's. It is holy to the Lord."* The tithe in this verse is described as holy. This means it is set aside for the Lord.

What this means is that when we receive our wages or income, the first 10% has already been designated as holy or belonging to God. We never have any rights over that 10% but in fact hold it for God (as it belongs to Him). If we spend that 10%, it is as if we were stealing it from God.

Yet the word "holy" is in fact the word "Cherem" in Hebrew. This means "accursed" or "destined for destruction". Thus the tithe is destined to be destroyed. If you try to hold onto it, you will find that it will disappear. I remember a time when I had forgotten to pay my tithe on a bonus I had received. For a period of a month, I found that certain kitchen appliances and 2 of my tyres on my car suddenly failed on me. Whilst kitchen appliances do have a natural life span and tyres likewise will occasionally burst, the occurrence of all of these within a short period of time was unusual. When my wife and I asked the Lord whether or not there was a cause, my mind was immediately drawn to the fact that I hadn't tithed part of my income.

This wasn't God's punishment for not tithing, it is simply that there is a principle that my 10% is already destined for destruction. If I try to hold onto it, it will not ultimately benefit me. God created the world with certain principles in place. One of those principles is the principle of the tithe. It is wisdom to understand and adopt the discipline of tithing.

The First Portion Redeems

There is a principle in the Bible that the first portion redeems the rest. In Romans 11:16 we read: "*For if the first fruit is holy, the lump is also holy; and if the root is holy so are the branches*". To redeem means to buy back and rescue. So by paying our tithe, we rescue the other 90% of our money.

Malachi 3:11 sets out some of the benefits of paying the tithe: "*And I will rebuke the devourer for your sakes, and he shall not destroy the fruits of your ground; neither shall your vine cast her fruit before the time in the field*" As we read in Genesis 3, the earth is cursed as a result of Adam's sin and producing food is difficult to do. In addition to this, the devil is looking to destroy and steal your possessions. One of the powerful benefits of the tithe is that it protects you from the schemes of the devil.

Every time we give our tithe, my wife and I pray the following: "Father, thank you for the benefits of the tithe. We thank you for rebuking the devourer over our finances and our household. We claim by faith the benefits of the tithe".

The promises of the Lord are to be accessed by faith and obedience. It is obedience to tithe, but that obedience must be combined with faith in the word of God in order to see the benefits of that word.

Prayer

Join me in prayer for your tithe:

"Father, thank you for the benefits of the tithe. We thank you for rebuking the devourer over our finances and our household. We claim by faith the benefits of the tithe"

Day 19 - Tithe (Part 3)

"Bring all the tithes into the storehouse, that there may be food in My house, And try Me in this; says the Lord of hosts "If I will not open for you the windows of heaven And pour out for you such blessing, That there will not be room enough to receive it". Malachi 3:10

The tithe requires faith. To give the first 10% of your income to God, not knowing what will happen in that month requires faith. This is why God says "try me in this" or other versions say "test me in this". The tithe is by its very nature a test.

All throughout the bible, 10 represents a test:

- 10 plagues that tested Egypt;
- 10 commandments;
- 10 tests of Israel in the wilderness;
- 10 virgins had prepared; and
- 10 days of testing in Revelation.

Yet when God says "try Me" he means it. The number of testimonies in our church alone of financial miracles and breakthrough that occur the moment someone starts to tithe and actively trusts God in this area are amazing. I remember looking at one lady's finances. She earned so little and had so many debts that I remember thinking "how can I suggest she tithes?" Yet I know that God honours those who honour Him. So we put in place a tithe in her life. Within a week there was release of provision to eliminate the biggest debt (which would have taken her over 1 year to pay off in small instalments). She has also learnt how to tap into divine provision for other areas of her life and is enjoying blessings well beyond the size of her pay cheque. Yet none of these blessings would have been realised had she not established the importance of the tithe in her life.

What does the tithe do? The verse makes it clear that the effect of tithes and offerings are to open up the windows of heaven. What does this mean? It means that the resources of heaven become available to you. The tithe gives you access to the resources of heaven, so you do not need to simply rely on your own resources. I have heard the tithe described as the fee that keeps your heavenly bank account open. Yet it is offerings that credit your account. This can be shown in the diagram below:

Tithe - Opening Bank Account

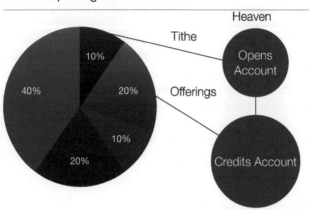

The tithe is the starting point of your giving and attracts huge benefits. Yet there are even greater benefits when you understand the power of offerings.

Practical Tips

- Set your tithe up as a direct debit from your bank account
- Make sure that the Church (and you) get any tax benefits that are available from giving your tithe
- Pray over your tithe when you give it - combine obedience with faith
- Believe God for protection of your life and family and that he will rebuke the enemy when you give the tithe
- Believe in faith your heavenly bank account is kept open by the tithe

Prayer

"Father, I want to live a life of faith in relation to my finances. I thank you that as I tithe the windows of heaven are opened over my life"

Day 20 - Offerings (Part 1 - Generosity)

The primary purpose for your money is to give it away to see the kingdom of God expand. In order to fulfil this purpose you have to grow in generosity.

Giving is Your Nature as a Believer

Our nature as believers is to be like God's nature. Salvation means that you are being transformed to be like our God. Our God is a generous god. In John 3:16 we see that God so loved the world that he gave. What he gave was his only son, Jesus. God couldn't have given anything more extravagant or more generous than his only son, Jesus. Our starting point is that God is absurdly generous and is calling us to be the same.

In Matthew 7:11, Jesus says *"If you, then, though you are evil, know how to give good gifts to your children, how much more will your Father in heaven give good gifts to those who ask him!"* What Jesus is saying is that if you think you are generous as a father, then you should take a look at God. By comparison to God you are an "evil" father. God is a God who wants to be known as giving "good gifts". No mediocre gifts, just good gifts.

We can see that the Holy Spirit is the same. In 1 Cor 12: 4 we read *"There are different kinds of gifts, but the same Spirit distributes them."* Just as God the father gives good gifts, the Holy Spirit also gives different kinds of gifts. God is simply generous. We as believers are also called to this lifestyle of outrageous generosity.

For some of us generosity is a heart issue. You need to either break free of the power of mammon in your life or the spirit of poverty. I would suggest you re-read the previous teaching on these issues and apply the principles set out in order to get your heart right. For others it is a capacity issue - you simply don't have the money to give. There may be extreme debt issues, employment issues or spending issues. In each case, the principles set out in this book will see you get out of these issues.

Types of Giving

There are many types of biblical ways in which you can demonstrate your generosity. The bible highlights the following:

The Tithe

"Bring the whole tithe into the storehouse, that there may be food in my house. Test me in this," says the Lord Almighty, "and see if I will not throw open the floodgates of heaven and pour out so much blessing that there will not be room enough to store it." Mal 3:10.

We considered this at length over the past three days.

Family

"For God said, 'Honor your father and mother' and 'Anyone who curses their father or mother is to be put to death.' But you say that if anyone declares that what might have been used to help their father or mother is 'devoted to God,' they are not to 'honor their father or mother' with it. Thus you nullify the word of God for the sake of your tradition." Matt15:5

I cannot claim to be a devout follower of Jesus if I prosper whilst my family are in rags. It is a sign of my devotion to God that I honour and protect my family with the income and wealth that I possess.

Sowing and Reaping

"Do not be deceived: God is not mocked, for whatever one sows, that will he also reap." Gal 6.

We will consider this topic in some detail in Section 3.

Poor/needy

"Whoever is kind to the poor lends to the Lord, and he will reward them for what they have done." Prov 19:17

The poor are close to God's heart. He promises that when we are kind or give to the poor, God will reward is for what we have done. An amazing example of this is in the life of Cornelius. We read in Acts 10:4: *"The angel answered, "Your prayers and gifts to the poor have come up as a memorial offering before God".* Cornelius was the first non-Jewish person to be saved. What qualified him for this honour? In part it was his gifts to the poor. God saw Cornelius' heart and decided to honour him in an amazing way. We cannot know what we qualify ourselves for with God when we bless the poor, but it is likely to be amazing.

Church/missions

Paul says in 2 Cor 8:2 that *"In the midst of a very severe trial, their overflowing joy and their extreme poverty welled up in rich generosity. For I testify that they gave as much as they were able, and even beyond their ability. Entirely on their own, they urgently pleaded with us for the privilege of sharing in this service to the Lord's people"*

We get the honour of sharing in missions by supporting them with our finances. Just imagine when you get to heaven and you can stand with the great evangelists of our time that you have helped support with money. God will give you credit for the souls won because you support them in missions.

Honouring others

"King Solomon gave the queen of Sheba all she desired and asked for, besides what he had given her out of his royal bounty" 1 Kings 10:13. There is a level of giving which goes beyond giving to meet needs. Solomon gave a gift to Queen of Sheba not because she needed it, but to honour her and to show who he, Solomon was.

We need to learn how to use our giving to honour others who are worthy of honour and reflect the power of the kingdom of God working within us. It is easy to give where you can see a need. It is only when we step into our place of kingship that we give to honour others.

Questions

Where do you currently give money to? Do you believe you

are generous? If not why not?

Are there any of those categories of giving that you are not currently involved in? If so which ones? How can you plan your giving differently?

Prayer

"Father, give me your heart for generosity"

Day 21 - Offerings (the benefits of Giving)

There are three levels of Giving that are found in the bible:

Three levels of Giving

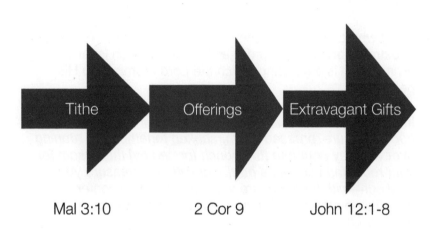

| Tithe | Offerings | Extravagant Gifts |
| Mal 3:10 | 2 Cor 9 | John 12:1-8 |

Tithes have already been discussed. Offerings are anything given over the tithe. The third category is extravagant gifts. This is demonstrated in John 12:1-8 which reads: *"Six days before the Passover, Jesus came to Bethany, where Lazarus lived, whom Jesus had raised from the dead. Here a dinner was given in Jesus' honor. Martha served, while Lazarus was among those reclining at the table with him. Then Mary took about a pint of pure nard, an expensive perfume; she poured it on Jesus' feet and wiped his feet with her hair. And the house was filled with the fragrance of the perfume.*
But one of his disciples, Judas Iscariot, who was later to betray him, objected, "Why wasn't this perfume sold and the money given to the poor? It was worth a year's wages." He did not say this because he cared about the poor but because he was a thief; as keeper of the money bag, he used to help himself to what was put into it.

"Leave her alone," Jesus replied. "It was intended that she should save this perfume for the day of my burial. You will always have the poor among you, but you will not always have me."

Other examples of extravagant giving are:

• King David saving billions for a temple he would never build;
• King Solomon sacrificing 1000 bulls to open the temple;
• The widow who gave 2 mites (all she had) into the offering at the temple.

Many who conquer the tithe move onto offerings. The level of extravagant gifts is harder again. Yet at each level of giving there is a blessing which the Lord promises to His people.

In Luke 6:38 we read: *"Give, and [gifts] will be given you, good measure, pressed down, shaken together and running over will they pour into [the pouch formed by] the bosom [of your robe and used as a bag]. For with the measure you deal out—with the measure you use when you confer benefits on others—it will be measured back to you. (Amplified)"*

When we give, we can legally expect God to bless us abundantly. We don't give to receive, but God has designed it so that your giving produces a harvest of blessing. Note that God always gives with purpose. God gave his only son for a purpose, that whoever believes in Jesus will be saved. God's heart was to see us reconciled to Him. He was willing to give the ultimate gift to secure that prize. God's giving yielded a harvest of blessing and we should expect that ours will also.

Matthew 6:19 reads: *"Do not store up for yourselves treasures on earth, where moths and vermin destroy, and where thieves break in and steal. But store up for yourselves **treasures in heaven**, where moths and vermin do not destroy, and where thieves do not break in and steal. For where your treasure is, there your heart will be also."* How do we store up treasures in heaven? Simply by giving to see the kingdom of God grow. We can often understand 'treasures in heaven" to mean something that we will only enjoy once we get to heaven. Yet Jesus promises his disciples in Mark 10:29-31 that whoever leaves "fields" (or sources of income) for the sake of Him will receive a 100 times in this life and in the life to come. The blessings of giving are for both now and in eternity.

Whilst many of us want to be blessed with a larger money assignment, it should be noted that God promises even more important blessings which he describes as "true riches" to those who can give their money to the kingdom of God (see Luke 16). It is interesting to note that the stewards who were given money to steward in Luke 19 were rewarded by influence over cities to reward their stewardship of small amounts of money. I firmly believe that revival in our cities and our nations are linked to our obedience in this area of money.

Questions

Just stop and think about the implications of your handling of money. What is your prayer for your community?

Do you give with purpose or simply give? Why?

Prayer

"Father, I want to get this issue of giving right in my life. I thank you that you promise blessings when I give. Lord I want to live in the fullness of your blessings"

Day 22 - Savings

"And he told them this parable: "The ground of a certain rich man yielded an abundant harvest. He thought to himself "What shall I do? I have no place to store my crops." Then he said " This is what I'll do. I will tear down my barns and build bigger ones and there I will store my surplus grain. And I'll say to myself, "You have plenty of grain laid up for years. Take life easy; eat, drink and be merry." But God said to him "You fool!" This very night your life will be demanded from you. Then who will get who you have prepared for yourself?" "This is how it will be for whoever stores up things for themselves but is not rich toward God". Luke 12:16

It is very easy to read this parable and conclude that savings are wrong. This would be the wrong conclusion! It is fair to say that those who trust in their own savings and investments as a means of living an easy life without pursuing the expansion of the kingdom of God through their money are not fulfilling their purpose in life and are not being "rich toward God". God wants you to live a life of faith in Him, not in the power of your savings. However, the principle of savings is wisdom within the context of your purpose.

After establishing the tithe, the next step to take in your finances is establishing an emergency saving fund. This would not be a large sum of money, but sufficient to cover, for example, the car breaking down or the boiler going wrong.

Proverbs 31:19 says the following about God *"How abundant are the good things that you have stored up for those who fear you that you bestow in the sight of all"* We can see that God himself saves. He stores up (or saves) "good things" in order to reward those who fear Him in public. If God saves for a good purpose, we also should do the same. The first aspect of saving is to save in order to be in a position to bless others with substantial gifts.

We can see this principle being applied in the life of Joseph. This is what he said to Pharaoh: *"Let Pharaoh appoint commissioners over the land to take a fifth of the harvest of Egypt during the seven years of abundance. They should collect all the food of these good years that are coming and store up the grain under the authority of Pharaoh, to be kept in the cities for food. This food should be held in reserve for the country, to be used during the seven years of famine that will come upon Egypt, so that the country may not be ruined by the famine." (Genesis 41:34-).* Joseph implemented a policy of saving which saved a nation from ruin and was also used to provide for and bless other neighbouring nations.

The second aspect of saving is to save for the expected. Proverbs 22:3 read *"A prudent man foresees difficulties ahead and prepares for them; the simpleton goes blindly on and suffers the consequences".* We know that things in life have a limited life expectancy yet often live as if they will last forever! Washing machines, cars, tyres, clothes, boilers etc. all require maintenance and eventually need replacing. Savings ensure that it is not a painful surprise when this happens.

The third aspect of savings is to prepare for large purchases. Proverbs 24:3-4 states that *"Any enterprise is built by wise planning, becomes strong through common sense, and profits wonderfully by keeping abreast of the facts".* In other words you need to plan for large purchases. When do you want to replace your car? When do you want to move house? These are questions which you need to discuss with God, but bear in mind that each of these moves may require money.

I would encourage you to make a list of when you would expect to have to replace some of the items in your home and how much this will cost. This will give you an idea of the amount of money you would need to save to replace these items without having to turn to debt.

The fourth aspect of savings is preparing for seasons in your life. Proverbs 6:6-8 reads *"Go to the ant, you sluggard; consider its ways and be wise! It has no commander, no overseer or ruler; yet it store its provisions in summer and gather its food at harvest".* There will be seasons in your life when you have more money and some where you may have less. Prepare for retirement or other times when your income is likely to be less.

One related issue to savings is insurance. Proverbs 27:12 reads *"A prudent man sees evil and hides himself, the naive proceed and pay the penalty"*. Insurance covers potentially large costs that you could not afford by yourself. Insurance is like the foundation of your house - not glamorous but you sure would miss it if it wasn't there! I would recommend that you consider taking out the following insurances as and when you can afford to do so:

1. **Home insurance** - this covers the items in your home in case of a fire or a burglary.

2. **Life insurance** - to provide cover for your family if you died.

3. **Critical illness cover -** this can often be expensive but may be worthwhile if you are the sole breadwinner for your family.

4. **Medical Insurance** - for those living without free healthcare in your country then medical insurance covers the cost of potentially expensive treatments.

With all insurance, I would suggest that you set your deductible (the amount you have to pay before the insurer will pay you) at a high level as this will reduce the amount the insurance will cost. Provided you have put some money aside in savings, high deductibles should not be a problem for you.

The question often arises whether or not taking out insurance or keeping savings is contrary to living in faith. I firmly believe that it is God's will for us to live in divine health and that healing has been paid for on the Cross. I firmly believe that it is God's heart to prosper us so we can fulfil our God given purpose.

However, I don't believe savings or insurance represents a lack of faith. Jesus never promises that nothing will go wrong in our lives - the apostles themselves were beaten (and no doubt unable to work for periods of time), robbed, executed and even ship- wrecked. It cannot be said that these men were not men of faith Using our resources to cover ourselves and our families for these situations is biblical. It is wisdom as opposed to a lack of faith.

Questions

Do you currently save? How much do you think you need to save in order to cover your potential costs - are you doing that now?

Have you put in place insurance in your life? If so, do you need to consider doing so and if so, what types of insurance?

Prayer

"Father, I pray that I never live with a reliance on savings but instead use wisdom to save in order to bless others and provide for my family"

Day 23 - Debt Repayment (Part 1 - The Price of Debt)

"For the Lord your God will bless you as he has promised, and you will lend to many nations but will borrow from none. You will rule over many nations but none will rule over you." Deuteronomy 15:6

The first question we must address in relation to debt is "Is debt sinful?". The short answer is no. It is clearly sinful to borrow money and not repay it (see Psalm 37:21 *"The wicked borrow and do not repay, but the righteous give generously)*, but borrowing money in itself is not sinful.

However, as believers we can often overlook the power of debt in our lives. Western culture is built around debt. It is so much a part of our lives that we can easily miss the real cost of debt, not only in our finances, but also in relation to the emotional and spiritual pressure it can exert on our lives.

Proverbs 22: 6 reads: "6. *Train up a child in the way he should go, and when he is old, he will not depart from it. 7. The rich rules over the poor and the borrower is servant to the lender.*" We often hear verse 6: "Train up a child...." but never connect it with the following verse "the borrower is servant to the lender". I believe that the author of the proverb was trying to make a simple point: it is wisdom to train a child to avoid debt as debt removes your freedom to rule yourself and means that you serve another. Debt creates a spiritual bondage which prevents you from being truly free. 2 Corinthian 3:17 reads " *Now the Lord is the Spirit, and where the Spirit of the Lord is, there is freedom.".* God is calling you to freedom. Debt destroys that freedom.

Proverbs 17:18 reads "*One who has no sense shakes hands in pledge and puts up security for a neighbour*". The bible describes guaranteeing the liabilities of another to be foolish. The reason being that you have no control over your neighbour's repayment and can lose your freedom through someone else's actions. I make it a policy in my life not to give guarantees for others. I would much rather bless others with large monetary gifts rather than enter into a guarantee arrangement on their behalf.

However, any form of debt comes at a cost. Haggai 1:6 *"You have sown much and bring in little. You eat, but you do not have enough. You drink, but you are not filled with drink. You clothe yourselves, but no one is warm. And he who earns wages, **earns wages to be put into a bag with holes**.'"* Debt is a bag with holes in it. The simple message is that debt causes you to lose money. If you are to be good stewards over God's money then debt is generally to be avoided. Certainly almost every form of consumer debt should be avoided.

By means of example, let us say that you borrowed £5,000 on credit cards to buy a sofa at an average interest rate of 18.9%. If you made minimum payments on this sum you would repay the debt in 31 years time and have paid interest of £7,076. So the total amount you would have repaid is £12,076. If you were asked whether or not you were willing to pay £12,000 for that sofa you would no doubt reply "no way" but yet that is exactly what you have ended up doing. So many people I speak to are simply making these kinds of minimum payments on their credit cards. They are literally putting their money in bags with holes! My advice to anyone who has a credit card but does not repay it in full every month (thus avoiding interest) is to cut it up. Yet nearly all debt carries a hidden price tag.

Most of us will be familiar with the account in Genesis of Adam and Eve. Eve and then Adam ate of the fruit which God told them not to eat. In Genesis 3:13 we read *"And the Lord God said to the woman, "What is this that you have done?" And the woman said, "The serpent **beguiled** me, and I ate.".* The word beguiled is the Hebrew word "Nasha". Nasha literally means to lend with interest. Adam and Eve took on a spiritual debt that they could not afford to repay. A debt that would cause huge levels of suffering for many generations. Interestingly, the word Nasha comes from a root word which is "Nashak" which means to be bitten by a poisonous snake. The Jewish people were in no doubt about the risks of debt. We often see health warnings on cigarettes, for the Jewish people the word "debt" carried a health warning: It *was* literally being described as being bitten by a snake.

Yet the biggest cost of any debt is the emotional pressure it can put you under. After having worked with people with debt issues, common themes arise:

- Debt makes you feel like you are powerless and drowning;

- People often end up working multiple jobs or huge amounts of overtime in order to meet demands;

- This puts a strain on family life as the mother or father are spending more time at work than at home and when they are at home their family are getting the worst of them;

- Debtors often try to hide from creditors (they don't open bills or ignore chasing calls). This makes the creditors even more aggressive and this causes them to pursue you with vengeance; and

- Aggressive debt chasers will often put pressure on the husband or wife of the debtor this creates huge pressures within the marriage.

Whilst we shall consider how to get out of debt, my advice is that if you are not currently in debt it should be generally avoided. Certainly all forms of consumer debt should be avoided at all cost. I would pray carefully about debt for purchasing a house or your business. Listen to see what God is saying to you. I know people who have successfully believed God for a debt free house and have seen that prayer answered. Certainly never borrow more than you can comfortably repay.

Questions

How have you treated debt? Have you avoided it or have you used it as part of day to day life? Why do you think this is the case?

Have you ever counted the true cost of that debt? Try doing a rough calculation of the price of your current debt.

Prayer

"Father, I want to be a good steward of the money you have given me. Give me grace in this area of debt."

Day 24 - Debt (Part 2 - Balance Sheet vs Cash Flow Statement)

"Whoever loves money never has enough; whoever loves wealth is never satisfied with their income. This too is meaningless." Ecc 5:10

The way in which we view our finances often deeply affects our spending habits. Most people see their finances as a cash flow statement. What do I mean by this? A cash flow statement looks at how much money I have coming in each month and how much I spend each month. You have already produced a cash flow statement for your money on day 14 (see Appendix 1)

A simple example of a Cash Flow Statement is below (this is for Mr Spender):

Income	Expenditure
£2,000 per month	Housing - £1,000
	Car - £250
	Food - £300
	Debt - £400

Many of us would look at Mr Spender's cash flow statement and say "I'm ok - I have £2,000 coming into my bank account but only spending £1,950. Great, there is £50 left over to spend or save".

On one view of life this is correct and most of us treat our finances in this manner. This is particularly so when a large percentage of Western income is tied up in debt. If you want a new car, you buy it in instalments paying interest on those instalments. If you want a new computer, you get a loan and repay it over a period of 2 years with interest. Thus the answer to any financial issue is more income in order to fund repayments.

The strength of a cash flow statement is that it shows you quickly if you are living a lifestyle beyond your means. Yet there is a real danger in seeing our finances only in this way: it hides your true financial position.

I would suggest that you also view your finances on a balance sheet basis. What is the balance sheet basis? It is a list of all of your assets (what you own) and all of your liabilities (what you owe). So the same person who had the cash flow statement above may well have a balance sheet that looks like this;

Assets	Liabilities
£200 cash	Credit Cards - £5,000
Jewellery - £1,500	Car loan - £3,000
	0% interest loans - £2,000
	Bills - £300

On a balance sheet basis Mr Spender has assets of £1,700 but liabilities of £10,300. On this basis, his financial position is far from healthy. He is, in fact, insolvent on a balance sheet basis. There are millions of people who appear to be doing well, but who are living their lives on the basis of a cash flow statement, yet if you actually looked at their assets and liabilities, they would be insolvent.

When we consider the area of debt, the cash flow statement only tells you how much you have to pay each month in order to service that debt, it hides the real value of the debt.

In order to address your debts, the first step is to work out how much you owe, to whom and at what rates of interest. Appendix 2 contains a table which will help you identify your debts. Take time to fill this properly.

From my experience, there can be a real reluctance in taking this step of looking at your debt. You can only bring something to God once you address it.

Questions

Do you think of your finances as a balance sheet or a cash flow statement? How does this affect the way you live?

Prayer

"Lord, I ask for grace to identify and deal with my debts. I ask for your help every step of the way."

Day 25 - Debt (Part 3 - Repayment Plans)

"And it shall come to pass, if thou shalt hearken diligently unto the voice of the Lord thy God, to observe and to do all his commandments which I command thee this day, that the Lord thy God will set thee on high above all nations of the earth: and all these blessings shall come on thee, and overtake thee, if thou shalt hearken unto the voice of the Lord thy God.... Thou shalt lend unto many nations, and thou shalt not borrow". (Deuteronomy 28: 1–2, 12)

The benefits of being out of debt cannot be overlooked. I set out below a worked example of benefits of repaying debts early. Each example is for a loan of £5,000 at a rate of 9.9% interest:

Period of Payment	Monthly Payment	Total Repaid	Total interest
10 years	£64.64	£7,756	£2,756
5 years	£104.95	£6,297	£1,297
3 years	£160.11	£5,764	£764
1 year	£438	£5,260	£260

The critical point to note is that the amount of money paid in interest is effectively lost money. The benefits of accelerated debt repayment are clear. You will have a lot more money to deal with and pursue your primary purpose (to give to the kingdom of God).

After establishing your tithe and a small emergency savings pot, the priority for your finances should always be debt elimination.

However, there is a question of which debt to repay first? I set out below my principles for debt repayment:

1. Authority Bills

Mark 12:17 reads "*Give back to Caesar what is Caesar's and to God what is God's.*" This is a clear direction from Jesus that the payment of taxes and government bills are important. This view is confirmed in Romans 13:1 which reads "*Let everyone be subject to the governing authorities, for there is no authority except that which God has established*"

Authority bills cover taxes, TV licence, car tax, council tax, benefits   repayments etc. You should ensure that these are addressed first. It may well be that you can reach an agreement for repayment with these authorities. If you can, then that is fine, however, ensure that you speak to these people first in order to agree repayments.

2.   Bills of necessity

Electricity, gas, water bills are your next priority. These are essential for living and either need to be dealt with or alternatively an agreement reached with them for repayment.

3.   Highest Interest Loans

After authority bills and bills of necessity, the bills you actually want to repay first are the highest interest bills. The more quickly you repay these bills the more money you will free up in order to address the other bills.

4.   Lower Interest Loans

These should be the last set of loans to deal with.

I should add a note about personal loans from family members or friends. Often these are given on an informal basis without any formal interest agreed on them and usually without any fixed repayment basis. However, they are rarely given without any expectations on the side of the lender. As time goes on these kinds of loans can form the basis of resentment and create all sorts of problems with the relationship. I would firstly recommend that any loans are properly structured with repayment dates and interest. If money is becoming an issue between family members, I would suggest repaying these in advance of the high interest loans.

I get those who see me to plan their debt repayment. The steps are as follows:

1. If you have money left after having finished the budget, savings and setting limits, this money should be used to create an emergency fund and immediately after that to repay debts.

2. Any items you sell should go into repaying debts.

3. Every debt you repay (or even partly repay) will release more free money. You must be disciplined and apply this money to repaying the rest of your debts.

4. Follow the list of priorities - this list corresponds with God's heart and when you pursue His heart you should expect blessings.

I encourage those who are planning repayment of their debts to set out their debts and see how long it will take them to repay them at an accelerated rate. I find that with most people, they may well be debt free within 7 years (including those with mortgage debt).

I have set out a table at Appendix 3 for you to fill in.

Prayer

"Lord help me address my debts. As I do my part in repaying what I am able to repay, I ask for supernatural aid in accelerating this debt repayment."

Day 26 - Investment

"The plans of the diligent lead to profit". Proverbs 21:5

God wants us to multiply in all that we do. His basic instruction to Adam and Eve was to *"be fruitful and multiply"* (Genesis 1:28). Mankind was designed to multiply. The parable of the stewards or talents makes it clear that God, the master, is expecting multiplication of whatever he gives us. Jesus only invested in disciples who were multipliers - we know this because the 12 disciples spread the good news of Jesus to multiple nations causing thousands to become Christians. Paul picks up this theme in his letter to Timothy. We read in 2 Timothy 2:2 *"The things which you have heard from me in the presence of many witnesses, entrust these to faithful men who will be able to teach others also"*. What is Paul saying? He is saying invest in people who will take what you have given them and teach it to others, thus multiplying the message.

God is no different in the area of money. He expects us to multiply what He has given us to steward. It is outside the scope of this book to provide specific investment advice (not least of which because I am not a qualified financial advisor), however, I will set out some basic principles for investment:

1. **Compound interest will destroy your money in relation to debt but will multiply your savings**

Let me give you a simple example. If you are 15 years old and you   decide to save 50 pence a day until the age of 60. If you could get a 10% rate of interest on your savings by the time you hit 60 you would have £1 million of savings. The total amount you would have actually saved is £8,213. Compound interest is a powerful tool for the saver. Yet the reverse is true in relation to debt.

So my first piece of investment advice is to repay your debts as quickly as you can. I consider repayment of my debts as my primary form of investment. Now repayment of debts may seem unnecessary in times of low interest where the cost of debt is relatively cheap. Yet interest rates rarely stay low for a long period of time and when they go up, the increased cost of your debt can easily become a major financial burden.

2. Anti-Inflationary Investments should form part of your investment portfolio

Inflation is the measure of how much prices go up in the economy. Inflation has the effect of destroying savings. The reason being is that if you could buy a loaf of bread for £1 at the beginning of the year but due to inflation it now costs £5, your savings can buy less in real terms than it could at the beginning of the year As such, any balanced investment portfolio should include some investments which are immune to inflation. The classic example of this is gold or silver. There is a global demand for gold and the price paid reflects this global market. Generally speaking gold will beat inflation. The same can be said for certain high end watches or even handbags. Yet careful research is required before investing in these type of products. I would generally say that you should invest no more than 15% of your investment portfolio in anti-inflationary products.

3. Spread Your Risk

In Ecc 11:2 it reads: *"Invest in seven ventures, yes, in eight; you do not know what disaster may come upon the land."* Do not fall into the trap of putting all your money in a single investment. Spread your risk by investing in multiple ventures.

4. Invest Do Not Trade

Many people fancy themselves as traders as opposed to investors. Traders are people who look to make quick advantage of varying prices in products. If this is your job fine, but if it is not your job then avoid the lure of making quick money - it is more likely than not that you will be several steps behind those people (and in many cases computers) who trade all the time. Look for long term stable growth.

5.   Only Invest in things you understand

There is always a temptation to invest in schemes which promise a large return. However, if you cannot explain how your investment makes its money to someone like you spouse DO NOT invest in it. If you are investing in a company, ensure you understand the product they make and see why people want to buy it.

6.   Invest in Companies with low levels of debt

If debt can destroy your personal finances, the same is true of companies also. Even very clever businessmen are caught out by overreaching themselves in the area of debt. Look at any companies you want to invest in and consider carefully what their debt profile is. Do not invest in them if their debt levels are high comparative to their income.

7.   Think Long Term Not Short

Do not think about getting rich quick. Think about long term safe and steady investments.

Take time to consider your investment profile. For those with debt it is fairly straight forward (eliminate that debt), however, for those who have eliminated your debt spend time carefully considering your investments. Take godly advice from experienced Christian businessmen or financial advisors.

Prayer

"Father give me wisdom in the area of investments. Give me grace to multiply in the area of finances"

Day 27 - Work Ethic

Proverbs is full of verses extolling the virtues of hard work. It is worth reviewing these as they contain key truths.

Proverbs 12:11 reads : *"Those who work their land will have abundant food, but those who chase fantasies have no sense."* We all know people who are chasing the next fantasy or get rich scheme. It is wisdom to get on and pursue your current assignment rather than merely dream about things you cannot obtain. This message is reinforced in Proverbs 14:23 reads: *"All hard work brings a profit, but mere talk leads only to poverty"*.

Proverbs 18:9 reads: *"One who is slack in his work is brother to one who destroys."* Not doing your work properly is likened to being related to a destroyer. The ultimate destroyer is the devil. Not being diligent in your work place is not godly (in fact it is the opposite!). There is a sobering message for the lazy in Proverbs 21:25 *"The craving of a sluggard will be the death of him"*. The desire to be lazy will destroy your life.

Yet the blessings of working well are clear to see in Proverbs 22:29 *"Do you see someone skilled in their work? They will serve before kings; they will not serve before officials of low rank."* If you want influence then the starting point is to work hard and be as skilled as you can be in your area of expertise. If you do so then you will serve before kings.

Connected to this issue of work ethic is honesty in your work.   Proverbs 10:13 reads: *"Kings take pleasure in honest lips; they value the one who speaks what is right."* Those in authority are looking for those who speak honestly in all areas of life. Proverbs 22:20 reads: *"Have I not written thirty sayings for you, sayings of counsel and knowledge, teaching you to be honest and to speak the truth, so that you bring back truthful reports to those you serve?"*. God loves honesty and straightforward dealing.

As believers you should be working hard for those you serve. You should act with absolute integrity. No stealing (or "borrowing") items from your work, no cheating on your taxes, no slacking off when you should be working, no abuse of sick days. God is constantly looking for opportunities to bless you, yet you can disqualify yourself from blessing by poor work ethic or a lack of honesty.

Questions

If you asked your work colleagues, would they say you were a hard worker? If not what can you do to change that?

Do you act with absolute integrity in your workplace and at home? If not, what must you change?

Prayer

"Father, give me grace to work well for you. Forgive me where I have been lazy or dishonest and give me the strength to serve you fully in my work place".

SECTION 3 - FAITH

Day 28 - Faith (Part 1 - God has given you everything)

"His divine power has given us everything we need for a godly life through our knowledge of him who called us by his own glory and goodness. Through these he has given us his very great and precious promises, so that through them you may participate in the divine nature, having escaped the corruption in the world caused by evil desires"
2 Peter 1:3

Faith is key to a believers life. Without it we cannot please God (Hebrews 11:6). As lovers of God, our heart's desire is to please Him.

Faith draws on the limitless resources of Heaven and draws them to Earth. Faith is one of the keys to release the kingdom of God onto Earth. Jesus demonstrated the perfect life of faith - he healed the sick, fed the 5000, released the demonised, walked on water and turned water into wine. Faith is key to seeing divine increase in the area of finances.

The verse from 2 Peter 1:3 is a roadmap to exercising faith for provision. We are going to explore the truths of this verse over the following days with a view to exercising faith in the area of finances.

He has given us everything

Peter is clear: God has already given us everything we need for a godly life. What is a godly life? It is a life that God wants us to live! It is a life of integrity and holiness but it is also a life of freedom and prosperity. It is a life of abundance in all things so that you are equipped for every good work (2 Cor 9). God has already given you a legal right to abundance in your life.

We explored this subject of legal entitlement briefly on day 12. By means of recap:

1. Wealth was created by God for man

In Haggai 2:8 we read *"the silver is mine and the gold is mine declares the Lord Almighty"*. God therefore is the owner of our wealth. Yet we read in Genesis 2:12 in relation to the Garden of Eden, *"The gold of that land is good."* In Genesis 2:15, Adam was to work and take care of the garden. He was put in charge of it. Thus Adam was put in charge of gold and silver resources.

2. Sin caused man to lose their rights to wealth

When Adam sinned, he gave away the rights to the resources and riches of this world. We can see this clearly in the temptation of Jesus in Luke 4: 5-7: *"The devil led him up to a high place and showed him in an instant all the kingdoms of the world. And he said to him, "I will give you all their authority and splendor; it has been given to me, and I can give it to anyone I want to. If you worship me, it will all be yours."* Note that the devil says that the splendour or the riches of the kingdoms of the world belong to the devil because "it has been given to me". Who gave him the riches? Adam did when he sinned. Note that Jesus does not correct the devil's understanding by saying "you don't own them". Instead Jesus emphasises the requirement to serve and worship the owner of the wealth (God) as opposed to its steward (the devil).

3. Jesus' death and resurrection has restored believer's rights to wealth

Through the death and resurrection of Jesus he has reclaimed the wealth of the world for his people. In Revelation 5:12 we read the following about Jesus: *"Worthy is the Lamb, who was slain, to receive power and **wealth** and wisdom and strength and honour and glory and praise"*. Jesus now has the legal right to the wealth of the world. Further he shares that right with believers. In Eph 2:6 we read *"And God raised us up with Christ and seated us with him in the heavenly realms **in** Christ Jesus"*. So Jesus has the right to all wealth and we are seated with Christ in Christ. So whatever belongs to Jesus also belongs to us as believers (as we are in Christ). We have a legal right to the wealth that belongs to Jesus.

If we have them why do we not see the wealth?

Let us imagine that I decide to give you a house. I would get the legal paperwork drawn up and get the house transferred into your name. It would then be yours. But you would get no benefit from the house unless you came to me and collected the keys, moved into the house and started to live in it.

I remember being told the very sad story of a lady who appeared to be homeless. She walked around London with a shopping trolley containing bags of her clothes. When she died it was discovered that she was a millionaire with a beautiful house in one of the most expensive parts of the city. She was simply not living in what she owned.

For many believers this is the position we are in. You have been given access to everything, yet live in none of it. We are like the rich lady owning riches we never use. For many they simply do not know how to access what God has already given them.

How do we access the "everything"?

For many believers the starting point for any prayer regarding provision is a pleading or bargaining with God to help them. Whilst this a natural reaction, God can rightly turn around and say "I have already given you what you are asking for - kindly access it!"

The verse states clearly how you access the "everything" he is promising: "through our knowledge of him". We need knowledge if we are to access what He has given us. In particular we need to have knowledge of how God works and how His kingdom works. In Matt 6:33 we read "*But seek first his kingdom and his righteousness, and all these things will be given to you as well*". Seeking first His kingdom includes understanding how His kingdom works.

Each kingdom has rules or laws which govern how that kingdom works. God's kingdom is no different. It operates on godly principles and rules. Once we understand these principles we can access the "everything" he has already given to us.

Questions

Do you live as if you have access to everything? If not, why not?

Do you bargain or plead with God for provision? If so why?

Prayer

"Father give me a knowledge of you and your kingdom that I may live in divine provision in my life"

Day 29 - Faith (Part 2 - Escaping the Corruption of the world)

His divine power has given us everything we need for a godly life through our knowledge of him who called us by his own glory and goodness. Through these he has given us his very great and precious promises, so that through them you may participate in the divine nature, having escaped the corruption in the world caused by evil desires"
2 Peter 1:3

Yesterday we looked at the first part of this passage and concluded:

1. God has given you everything you need for a godly life;
2. a godly life is a life which includes abundance; and
3. the way in which we access this abundance is through a knowledge of God and His kingdom.

Escaping Corruption

Today we look at the second sentence of this verse. The exciting part of this verse is the promise that we can escape the corruption in the world. What is the corruption in the world that we get to escape? The corruption occurred when Adam sinned. The perfect creation became subject to sickness, poverty and a curse on the very ground of the earth (Gen 3).

Yet the promise is that we get to escape this corruption of poverty and sickness through the power of Jesus' death and resurrection. In giving us everything, the curse of poverty and lack is broken over our lives. If we live in the reality of "everything" the corruption of the world cannot touch us.

If we live in the light of this truth, we will live differently from the world. This corrupt world is built on the essential idea that there are limited resources and I need to make sure I have my fair share (and more) of them. God is saying that there are not limited resources for believers.

If I go to a restaurant buffet, I am not jealous of the large gentleman in front of me who has loaded his plate to the brim. Why? Because I know the restaurant will replace the food he has taken and I can have as much as I can manage. His consumption will not rob me of my fill of food. This is the attitude that God is looking to instil in believers. If we are entitled to everything, there should be no petty jealousies or desire to be in someone else's shoes.

The Promises

in order to obtain an escape from the corruption of the world we must do something. We must "participate". To be precise we must participate in the "divine nature". What does this mean? Well, we all have a human nature - this is the natural way humans do things. We eat, drink, sleep in a very similar way. We react as humans in very similar ways. This is human nature: doing what humans do.

Divine nature by contrast is doing things the way that God does them. In order to escape the corruption of the world we need to do things the way that God does them not the way humans do them.

We participate in the divine nature through the "precious promises". What the verse is saying is that we need to act like God does in relation to His precious promises. How do we do this?

Romans 4:17 is referring to Abraham and reads "*As it is written: "I have made you a father of many nations." He is our father in the sight of God, in whom he believed—the God who gives life to the dead **and calls into being things that were not**.*" God's nature is to call things into being that "were not". When we get a promise, we get to participate in the divine nature in that we get to call into being things that are not.

So every promise of God is an opportunity for us to walk in divine nature by saying that what God has promised is true (even though we do not yet see the fruit of that promise). When we participate in the divine nature in this way we get to escape the corruption of the world and access the "everything" that God has given us.

If I give you a cheque for £1,000 your response tells me a lot about your faith in me. A cheque is not money - it is the promise of money. For some of you who know me, if I give you a cheque for £1,000 you will start to plan how you can spend that money. Some of you will start ordering goods online knowing that in 3 days you will have the money in your account to meet those orders. You know that I would not promise you money and not pay it. You also are aware that I am able to honour a cheque for £1,000. The promise of £1,000 has formed an image in your heart of what you will receive. That image is so real that you will act on it now even though the money has not yet hit your bank account.

For others of you, you say "when I see it I will believe it!" You will not spend it or act on it until that money is sitting in your account.

These represent the two responses to God's promises. If you believe God's promises and have faith in Him, you will have a picture in your heart of the promise and will live as if that picture was real. You will act, speak and behave in every way as if the promise were true. This is what it is to participate in the divine nature.

The alternative is to doubt the word, waiting for absolute proof before believing the promise. This is living without faith. You do not participate in the divine nature unless you live in faith for the promises of God.

Faith is being in complete agreement with the promise of God. Not just mentally, but your heart is settled and convinced completely by what God promised. Faith occurs where our hearts and mind are in complete agreement with heaven and our hearts are fully persuaded, confident and at rest in the promises of God.

Tomorrow we will consider how to grow in faith.

Questions

Can you recall an instance when you fully believed a promise of God? What did it feel like?

Prayer

"Father, thank you for your precious promises. Thank you that each promise is an opportunity or invitation to participate in the divine nature by calling those things that are not as if they were. I declare that I want to live free from the corruption of this world."

Day 30 - Faith (Part 3 - Growing Faith)

"He also said, "This is what the kingdom of God is like. A man scatters seed on the ground. Night and day, whether he sleeps or gets up, the seed sprouts and grows, though he does not know how. All by itself the soil produces grain— first the stalk, then the head, then the full kernel in the head. As soon as the grain is ripe, he puts the sickle to it, because the harvest has come." Mark 4:26-29

Over the past 2 days we have concluded:

1. God has given us everything (including abundance);
2. You access this abundance through a knowledge of God and His kingdom;
3. You get to escape the poverty of this world by participating in the divine nature;
4. The divine nature involves speaking those things that are not as if they are;
5. Every promise in the Bible gives you an opportunity to participate in the divine nature by speaking the promise as if it were true (even though you do not see it);
6. In order to participate in the divine nature you need faith.

As such your ability to access the "everything" that God has for you depends on (i) having a promise; (ii) exercising faith in relation to the promise. Today we will look at how to see your faith grow.

The short parable in Mark 4:26-29 is packed with amazing truth about how faith works. We will consider it in small pieces:

A man scatters seed on the ground...

This parable follows immediately after the parable of the sower and the seed. This is good news as Jesus explains to his disciples what the "seed" represents and what the "ground" represents.

The seed is the word of God. A seed has the ability to create plants after its kind. So a seed of wheat has the ability or potential to create wheat. In the same way the living word of God has the ability or potential to create what it promises. If you take a word of God regarding peace it has the ability or potential to create peace in your life.

The ground is defined as the heart of a man or woman. Every word of God has to be planted in a person's heart. This means it cannot simply be a mental agreement to a word, it must go deep into our life and be allowed to change the way we think and live.

Night and day, whether he sleeps or gets up, the seed sprouts and grows

It is important to note that only three ingredients are needed to see faith grow in your life. The first is the word of God (the seed). The second is a heart that receives that word and holds onto that word (the soil). The third ingredient is time (night and day). We often think that there needs to be some mysterious fourth ingredient to make faith grow. There isn't. God created your heart to respond to the word of God so as to create faith. It is the interaction of your heart and the word of God that creates faith.

All by itself the soil produces grain....

Provided the word of God is kept and cherished in your heart, that word will begin to produce after itself. Increasingly you will see your life through the lens of the promise. Your current circumstances will appear to be less real in light of the faith that is growing in your heart based on the living word of God.

Eventually you will reach the point that every time you think about that area of your life all you can see in your mind is the truth of the promise. You will be so fully convinced about the promise that everything else fades into insignificance. This is when the plant is fully grown. This is when your faith has fully matured. This is the day you were waiting for!

However, having full faith in not enough! What I hear you cry - how can faith not be enough?

As soon as the grain in ripe, he puts the sickle to it

In order to enjoy the crops that a farmer has grown he must "put a sickle to them" or in other words he must do something to harvest those crops. In the same way in order to enjoy the benefits of our faith we must do something to harvest that faith.

Let me give you a biblical example: In Romans 10:10 it reads: *"For it is with your heart that you believe and are justified and it is with your mouth that you confess and are saved"*. In order to be saved, belief is not enough. You must also "confess" or in other words declare (or speak out) what you believe in your heart.

This is the same for every promise of God. Simply believing in your heart is not enough. You need to take an action based on your faith. It may be a confession, it may be another form of action. You must do something that demonstrates what you believe.

I have over the years experienced a lot of believers who make bold declarations and nothing happens. Why is this the case? There is no point in harvesting your wheat until it is mature. In the same way, confession without faith is unlikely to yield much fruit.

Prayer

"Father, let your promises capture my heart so that I may grow in faith in all areas of my life"

Day 31 - Putting it all together

"For no matter how many promises God has made, they are "Yes" in Christ. And so through him the "Amen" is spoken by us to the glory of God." 2 Cor 1:20

This amazing verse in 2 Corinthians makes a simple point. No matter how many promises God has made, the answer is always the same "yes". Why is the answer "yes"? Because of what Jesus has done. Our response then is to say "amen" or "I agree" with what Jesus has done. This is what we are called to do in our life, simply agree with the promises set out in His word.

Today we are going to explore step by step how to see the promises in God's word materialise in your life. This is a model of prayer I use. It is not a magic formula, but instead a series of steps based on scripture which have been proven time and again. It is not the only way to pray for provision, but is a good starting point:

1. **Step 1 - Identify Your Need**

This may seem simple, yet it is important that we specifically identify exactly what we want God to provide for us. Do not start with £1million! Most of us would not know what to do if we suddenly gained access to that sum of money and secondly if you are starting this process you are highly unlikely to have faith for £1 million. Start with you most immediate need. It may be a bill that needs paying, a school uniform that needs to be purchased, it may be your next meal.

I would always recommend you write down that need.

2. **Step 2 - Find a promise in the Bible that meets your need**

The provision of God is accessed through the "precious promises" of God. I have set out below some key promises of God for you to use:

Verses For Provision

Philippians 4:19: *"And this same God who takes care of me will supply all your needs from his glorious riches, which have been given to us in Christ Jesus."*

Proverbs 10:22: *"The blessing of the Lord makes a person rich, and he adds no sorrow with it."*

2 Corinthians 9:8: *"And God will generously provide all you need. Then you will always have everything you need and plenty left over to share with others."*

Jeremiah 17:7-8: *"But blessed are those who trust in the Lord and have made the Lord their hope and confidence. They are like trees planted along a riverbank, with roots that reach deep into the water. Such trees are not bothered by the heat or worried by long months of drought. Their leaves stay green, and they never stop producing fruit."*

Verses for Jobs

Psalm 90:17 *"May the favor of the Lord our God rest on us; establish the work of our hands or us yes, establish the work of our hands."*

Verses for Housing

Isaiah 32:18 *"My people will live in peaceful dwelling places, in secure homes, in undisturbed places of rest."*

There are hundreds of verses in the Bible in relation to specific types of provision. Keep reading until the Holy Spirit highlights one of the verses to you. Then meditate on that word. Write out the word and put it in places you can read.   Read it as many times as you can. You want your heart to be set on that word so that all you see when you think about your situation is that word. As discussed yesterday, you want a picture in your heart and mind which reflects perfectly the word of God.

3. **Step 3 - Make a Declaration**

God has already given you the provision you need, you simply need to access it. So we do not ask God for provision (I repeat - he has already given it to us). Instead we declare the promise of God. So your declaration could be "Lord I declare that you will supply all my needs according to your glorious riches. Based on that word I access, by faith, in the name of Jesus [my shopping for this week]."

We stand on the promise and agree with the promise.

4. **Step 4 - Rebuke the Devil off your provision**

The devil's job is to "steal kill and destroy" (John 10:10). With this in mind he is likely to want to intercept your provision. As such, we simply exercise the authority we have in Christ to rebuke the enemy over the provision that God has promised. I would therefore pray: "In the name of Jesus, I rebuke the enemy over my provision and command it to be released"

5. **Step 5 - Ask for God to commission angelic help**

Hebrews 1:14 "*Are not all angels ministering spirits sent to serve those who will inherit salvation?*" The role of angels is to serve believers. As such, they can also play a role in helping with your provision. Why would they care about your provision? Partly because many of us fail to serve God fully because we are so busy trying to put food on our tables. Now I do not accept that it is biblical to give angels orders and certainly not worship them, however, I do believe that they are here to serve us. I would therefore pray as follows: "Lord Jesus, please release angels on my behalf to gather the provision I need".

6. **Step 6 - Look for Your Provision**

You need to realise that all the provision you need is already on the earth. Heaven does not print money and put it in your lap! We can see this principle explained in Luke 6:38 which reads (in King James version) *"Give, and it shall be* *given unto you; good measure, pressed down, and shaken together, and running over, shall <u>MEN</u> give into your bosom.".* God uses men (and women) to bring you the provision you need. All of the wealth you need is already in the earth and God will direct you to it.

How does He do this? A very useful starting point was compiled by Wendell Smith in his manual "Prosperity with a Purpose". I have slightly amended it to make the list you see below:

- Jobs, better jobs and promotions, raises, bonuses and benefits
- Sales, commission increase, business opportunities
- Estates, settlements and inheritance
- Rebates, returns and cheques in the mail
- Scholarships and favour
- Interest and Royalties and insurance payments
- Gifts, surprises and finding money
- Wisdom & self-control in spending
- Bills decrease and income increase

Your provision is likely to come in one of these forms. It is important to look for how God is going to bless you.

I remember when I followed this procedure for £200. A couple of days later I was reviewing my insurance payments and realised that I was overpaying for my car insurance. Whilst I had to pay £50 to change insurers, I managed to get a £50 Amazon voucher from my new insurer and at the same time save almost £300. I therefore received the provision I was looking for.

Prayer

Your prayer today is the prayer of faith for provision. Follow the steps set out above.

Day 32 - Sowing and Reaping - Part 1

"When Jesus heard what had happened, he withdrew by boat privately to a solitary place. Hearing of this, the crowds followed him on foot from the towns. When Jesus landed and saw a large crowd, he had compassion on them and healed their sick.
As evening approached, the disciples came to him and said, "This is a remote place, and it's already getting late. Send the crowds away, so they can go to the villages and buy themselves some food."
Jesus replied, "They do not need to go away. You give them something to eat."
"We have here only five loaves of bread and two fish," they answered.
"Bring them here to me," he said. And he directed the people to sit down on the grass. Taking the five loaves and the two fish and looking up to heaven, he gave thanks and broke the loaves. Then he gave them to the disciples, and the disciples gave them to the people. They all ate and were satisfied, and the disciples picked up twelve basketfuls of broken pieces that were left over. The number of those who ate was about five thousand men, besides women and children." Matthew 14:13-21

This passage has made a huge impact on my life and has redefined the way in which I approach the issue of provision.

It was April 2016. My wife and I had sat down together and had drawn up a list of things we wanted to purchase and do. They included buying a tent so we could go to a Christian camping event, a shed to store our tools which were getting damaged, a holiday, new windows and doors for parts of the house which were not doing a great job of keeping the cold winter air out of the house. We also had computers that had stopped working or were seriously playing up. I was trying to work out how I could manage to afford all of these things. It is amazing how much pressure you can feel trying to work out your own finances. I came to the conclusion that I could only do this with a bonus (and a sizeable one at that). Bonus time was the end of April and so I waited with anticipation for the announcement. The announcement came on time - no bonus!

It was at this time that God was talking to me about the passage from Matthew 14:13-21 and was revealing to me keys to living in divine provision. To cut a long story short, that year we saw provision for everything on our list and in the process of doing this managed to radically increase our giving to the church and to others. What I am going to share with you over the following days not only brought our family all the blessings we were looking for but it has also completely removed the pressure from me in feeling that I have to sort out the finances in the household and make provision happen. There are so many people living under this pressure of having to provide. This is a pressure I don't believe God intended us to live under.

The account of the feeding of the 5000 is an amazing miracle of divine provision. Yet there are keys in this passage that can be applied to our lives to see God move miraculously in our own lives. I use these principles for all of the major areas of provision I need. I shall break this passage down into five stages which we will explore in more depth over the following days:

Stage 1 - Identifying a Need

The first thing that Jesus did was to identify what he wanted. He said to his disciples "you give them something to eat". Jesus had decided that he wanted to feed 5000 men as well as women and children. The first step is to identify what you are looking for God to do.

Stage 2 - Sow What You Have

Jesus then took what he had (being 5 loaves and 2 fishes) and he offered them to God. This is stage 2 - sow what you have.

Stage 3 - Give Thanks

Jesus takes the loaves and the fishes and he prays. The passage says that Jesus gave thanks for the 5 loaves and 2 fishes. Consider this, Jesus gave thanks well before the miracle happened. This is stage 3 - give thanks before you receive your provision.

Stage 4 - Believe Before You Receive

Jesus demonstrated his faith in God's provision. He sat the people down in groups in expectation. He broke the bread and gave it to his disciples to distribute. All of these acts were taken before there had been any multiplication of the bread and fish. Stage 4 requires you to move in faith for your provision before you receive it.

Stage 5 - He blesses the work of your hands

It was only as the disciples began to hand out the bread and fish that the multiplication happened. God always chooses to bless your work. He is not in favour of simply giving out handouts he wants you to be part of the process.

Conclusion

What we can see from this passage that Jesus combines two powerful spiritual laws. The first is the power of faith. The second is the principle of sowing and reaping. We are going to explore how to combine these powerful biblical truths together in order to see supernatural provision in your life.

I have set out a table at Appendix 5. I would encourage you to use this table for every area of provision you need. I will refer to this table over the following days.

Day 33 - Sowing and Reaping (Part 2 - Identifying the Need)

"You want something but you don't get it. You kill and covet but you cannot have what you want. You quarrel and fight. <u>You do not have because you do not ask God"</u> James 4:2

Stage 1 is identifying the need.

The verse in James is amazing, yet so true. I have often seen people make barbed comments about others who have either a nice house, a nice car or even go on nice holidays. Yet James is pretty clear on the reason. "You do not have because you do not ask God". The starting point for anything you need or want in life is to ask God for it! You would have thought that this was the simplest thing for any believer to do, yet I see time and time again people try to muddle through their issues hoping that somehow there will be a divine intervention at some point.

God wants to be involved in every aspect of your life and wants you to talk to him about the things that are on your heart. Yet in my experience there are a number of reasons why believers do not go to God:

1.   **Guilt/shame** - often people have got themselves into a mess with their finances through making foolish decisions. There is shame associated with the mess. As such, they don't feel able to approach God and ask for grace.

Romans 10:11 reads as follows: "As Scripture says, *"Anyone who believes in him will never be put to shame.""* God does not want your shame to get in the   way of your provision.

2.   **Belief Systems** - often believers get very worried about asking God for things that are not "life and death" needs, in case they are being guilty of greed. A lot of people have asked me if it is ok to sow for a holiday or a car etc. In almost every case these people are generous, God fearing, non-materialistic people. Yet they have in their head this notion that you cannot ask God for nice things. This is a lie. It is a way of thinking that sounds correct but

robs your life of transforming power.

I know that God cares about my heart's desires. When I sowed for a tent, I didn't sow for the cheapest most efficient tent I could sow for. No, I told God exactly the type of tent I wanted. I wanted one that I could blow up using air to save time in putting it up and putting it down. Were these tents more expensive - yes! Was it the one that I wanted - yes! Does God care about what bothers me - yes!

Now God does not honour excessive consumption or materialism. This is why James 4:3 reads: "*When you ask, you do not receive, because you ask with wrong motives, that you may spend what you get on your pleasures.*" However, there is a large gap between the kind of excessive consumption that James is talking about and the average believer who would like a holiday or a car that is reliable.

3.   **Self-sufficiency** - it is fair to say that those who come to the Lord in the area of their money do need to recognise the Lordship of God over their finances. Many people realise the irony of trying to run their finances themselves and then coming to God when it goes wrong. As a result people do not go to God because they do not want to submit to God's authority in this area of their life. Yet as with the prodigal son, your money taken outside of the Lordship of God will be of no eternal value. Now is the time to stop being self-sufficient and instead be God-sufficient.

God Answers Prayer!

John 14:13 reads "*And I will do whatever you ask in my name, so the Son may bring glory to the Father. You may ask anything in my name, and I will do it*".

Matthew 7:7- reads: "*Ask and it will be given to you; seek and you will find; knock and the door will be opened to you. For everyone who asks receives; the one who seeks finds; and to the one who knocks, the door will be opened. "Which of you, if your son asks for bread, will give him a stone? Or if he asks for a fish, will give him a snake? If you, then, though you are evil, know how to give good gifts to your children, how much more will your Father in heaven give good gifts to those who ask him!*"

Matthew 21:22 reads *"If you believe, you will receive whatever you ask for in prayer."*

John 16:24 reads *"Until now you have not asked for anything in my name. Ask and you will receive, and your joy will be complete."*

The point I am making is simple. The Bible is full of promises that God answers prayer. God promises that he is a good father who is longing to bless His children with what they need and even what they want in life. However, the most important thing to note is that each of these passages full of promises starts with you asking!

How to ask....

This may appear to be an odd heading but it is important. When I start to ask for God's provision, I fill in the "seed name" column of the table at Appendix 5. Here are my tips for asking God for provision:

1.   ***Be very specific*** - tell God exactly what you want. If there is a brand or model you want, tell him what you want. It is amazing how much your faith grows when you see the way that God moves to bring you the precise thing you sowed for.

2.   ***Don't Assume Money is always the answer*** - if you want a loan to be cancelled or repaid, then sow for the cancellation or repayment of the loan. Do not assume that the only way God can answer your prayer is through the money to repay the loan. The same is true for everything else - if you want say a phone, ask for a phone. Do not assume that the only way God can bring you that phone is through money. It is really exciting seeing the way in which God brings your provision.

3.   ***Do not ask for more than you have faith for -*** starting with the repayment of your mortgage in full may well be what you want first, but honestly ask yourself if you have faith for that. Start by finding God faithful in the smaller things and   see your faith grow to greater levels.

4.   **If you are married, make sure your request is agreed** - In 1 Peter 3:7 we read: *"Husbands, in the same way be considerate as you live with your wives, and treat them with respect as the weaker partner and as heirs with you of the gracious gift of life, so that nothing will hinder your prayers.".* You will see here that prayers can be hindered where there is a discord between husband and wife. This is not surprising as God declares that when a man and woman become married they are "one flesh". God sees you as one. So if part of you says "I want something" but the other part of you says "no" there is a tension! My wife and I make it a policy not to ask for anything unless the other person is on board with that request.

So you can now start to fill in your requests to God in column labelled "Seed Name".

Prayer

"Father, may I come to you for all I need in life. Thank you for your amazing promises of provision. I come into agreement with those promises and ask you for provision"

Day 34 - Sowing and Reaping (Part 3 - Sowing)

"the point is this: whoever sows sparingly will also reap sparingly, and whoever sows bountifully will also reap bountifully." 2 Cor 9:6

Stage 2 of this process is sowing a seed.

The verse from 2 Corinthians above refers to an important biblical principle of sowing and reaping. The image used is of a farmer who sows seed into the ground and in time will reap a harvest. The message of this scripture is clear, a farmer who sows only a small amount of seed will only reap a small harvest yet a farmer who sows a lot of seed will have a large harvest.

This verse is not the only reference to sowing and reaping. The New Testament makes a number of references to sowing and reaping. I set out below some of the key verses in this area:

Gal 6:7 *"Do not be deceived: God is not mocked, for whatever one sows, that will he also reap."*

Luke 6:38 *"Give, and it will be given to you. Good measure, pressed down, shaken together, running over, will be put into your lap. For with the measure you use it will be measured back to you."*

The blessings associated with sowing and reaping are an extension of the blessings that flow from generosity which we considered in day 20. There is a promise that as you sow or give into the lives of others you will receive a harvest in proportion to that which has been sowed. In seeking God's provision we are going to be combining faith with the powerful principles of sowing and reaping.

Today we are going to set out the basics of sowing and reaping and tomorrow we will look at how much to sow.

What is the difference between giving and sowing?

My wife and I are not very strong gardeners. When we were looking to introduce flowers to our flower bed, my wife took a packet of assorted wildflower seeds and sowed them into the ground. The result was that we had a random assortment of flowers growing. The seeds we sowed resulted in flowers growing, but we had no idea of what exactly we would get. This is a picture of general giving or generosity. When we give to to others, it is like sowing assorted seeds. We know that we will get a blessing on our giving, but we are not sure what that harvest of blessing will be.

By contrast a farmer never sows assorted seeds in his fields. He decides in advance what he wants to grow. If he wants to grow wheat he sows wheat seeds. If he wants to grow barley, he sows barley seeds. If he wants apples, he sows apple seeds. This is a picture of sowing and reaping. It is a specific type of giving where we specifically define what we want to see as a result of our giving. By means of example, if you want money to meet a bill, you can sow specifically for money for that bill.

Seeds replicate themselves

In nature, seeds replicate themselves. This is why apple seeds can only produce apple trees. The same is true in relation to biblical sowing and reaping. So when I was asking God for a new watch, I started by sowing my best watch.

This principle is reflected in Matthew 5:7 which reads: *"Blessed are the merciful, for they will be shown mercy."* So those who sow mercy will reap mercy. So if you are in need of mercy in your life the most sensible thing to do is to show mercy to those who have wronged you.

So what happens if you don't have something of the same type to sow? If you are sowing for a car and you don't have a car to sow what can you do? The short answer is you can use money. Money is a universal trading instrument. If you go to the car show room and want to obtain a car, you can use money to buy that car. In the same way money can be used instead of almost any item when it comes to sowing.

As such, when we sow for provision, you can always sow using money.

Are we simply trying to buy God's provision?

Let me be clear, you cannot buy God's blessing. The only way to access the provision of God is faith in His word. When we sow and reap we are accessing by faith the promises of God and using the kingdom principles of sowing and reaping through faith.

No one would ever accuse a farmer when he is sowing his wheat seeds of "buying" the wheat harvest. Instead you would say that the farmer is observing the laws of nature, knowing that if he sows seeds, in time there will be a harvest. The farmer must trust the laws of nature when he takes precious seeds and put them in the ground.

In the same way, as believers, we can observe the laws of the kingdom of God knowing that as we sow we will also reap a harvest. Yet we must trust the laws of God's kingdom and more importantly have faith in the power of God to trust Him when we sow our money into His kingdom we will reap a harvest.

What can I sow?

As the tithe belongs to God, you cannot sow your tithe. You cannot sow something which belongs to another. As such, you can sow from your offerings but not from your tithe.

Where should I sow?

You sow where God tells you to. I would generally recommend that you sow into a church or believers who share your faith for God's provision.

Prayer

"Father, help me understand and enjoy the blessings of sowing and reaping"

Day 35 - Sowing and Reaping (Part 4 - How much)

"One day as Jesus was standing by the Lake of Gennesaret, with the people crowding around Him and listening to the word of God. He saw at the water's edge two boats, left there by the fishermen who were washing their nets. He got into one of the boats, the one belonging to Simon, and asked him to put out a little from shore. Then He sat down and taught the people from the boat. When He had finished speaking, He said to Simon. "Put out into the deep water, and let down the nets for a catch." Simon answered, "Master, we've worked hard all night and haven't caught anything. But because You say so, I will let down the nets." When they had done so, they caught such a large number of fish that their nets began to break. So they signaled their partners in the other boat to come and help them, and they came and filled both boats so full they began to sink. When Simon Peter saw this, he fell at Jesus' knees and said, "Go away from me, Lord; I am a sinful man!" For he and all his companions were astonished at the catch of fish they had taken, and so were James and John, the sons of Zebedee, Simon's partners... (Luke 5: 1-10)"

We are continuing our study on sowing. Yesterday we established the following:

1. sowing and reaping is a biblical principle which replicates nature;
2. sowing is giving with a view to seeing a specific blessing from God as opposed to the general blessing of generosity;
3. it is only faith in God which will access the promises of God but by combining your faith with sowing, you are enjoying the combined benefits of faith and the principle of sowing; and
4. you can sow money for all types of blessings, but you cannot sow your tithe as it belongs to God.

Today we are going to consider the question of how much should I sow?

Did you know that you can limit your blessings of provision? Consider the account above. We can see that Simon received instructions from Jesus to go into the deep water and put down his nets. Simon did not appreciate the significance of what Jesus was saying, nor the level of blessing he was going to receive. Had Simon simply said "no thanks - I am way too tired", he would have received no blessing. Yet Simon was obedient and did as Jesus said. The result was a harvest which was so big that Simon needed to call in his partners to help. The bible says that they filled "both boats so full that they began to sink". What would have happened if they had not a few boats, but hundreds of boats? More likely than not, the blessing would have been even more amazing. The blessing of the miracle was limited to the number of boats available to collect the harvest.

There is a similar principle shown in 2 Kings 4:1-7: "*The wife of a man from the company of the prophets cried out to Elisha, "Your servant my husband is dead, and you know that he revered the Lord. But now his creditor is coming to take my two boys as his slaves." Elisha replied to her, "How can I help you? Tell me, what do you have in your house?" "Your servant has nothing there at all," she said, "except a little oil." Elisha said, "Go around and ask all your neighbors for empty jars. Don't ask for just a few. Then go inside and shut the door behind you and your sons. Pour oil into all the jars, and as each is filled, put it to one side." She left him and afterward shut the door behind her and her sons. They brought the jars to her and she kept pouring. When all the jars were full, she said to her son, "Bring me another one." But he replied, "There is not a jar left." Then the oil stopped flowing. She went and told the man of God, and he said, "Go, sell the oil and pay your debts. You and your sons can live on what is left*".

The widow in this story was in trouble. She owed money and had no means of repaying it. She came to the prophet of God asking for help. Elisha started by asking her what she had. She replied that she had a little oil. Note that as with sowing and reaping, God will use what you have for supernatural increase. He then told her to gather empty jars from her neighbours. She did this and then the miracle of supernatural increase in oil occurred. Note that the oil kept increasing until she ran out of jars. What would have happened if she had say 1 million jars? The oil would have kept going until she had filled all of those jars. What limited the level of the blessing the widow received? The number of jars she had. She had herself defined the level of blessing she was going to receive by the number of jars she had gathered.

We see another example of this again in 2 Kings 13:16: *"Elisha said, "Get a bow and some arrows," and he did so. "Take the bow in your hands," he said to the king of Israel. When he had taken it, Elisha put his hands on the king's hands."Open the east window," he said, and he opened it. "Shoot!" Elisha said, and he shot. "The Lord's arrow of victory, the arrow of victory over Aram!" Elisha declared. "You will completely destroy the Arameans at Aphek."Then he said, "Take the arrows," and the king took them. Elisha told him, "Strike the ground." He struck it three times and stopped. The man of God was angry with him and said, "You should have struck the ground five or six times; then you would have defeated Aram and completely destroyed it. But now you will defeat it only three times."*

Here we have a king who was asked to shoot arrows out of the window. The king did not know why he was shooting the arrows out of the window, simply that the prophet of God had asked him to do so. So when the king shot the arrows out of the window as asked to do so by Elisha, he only shot 3 arrows. Elisha is cross. He makes it clear that there was a link between the number of arrows the King shot and the level of victory he would have over his enemies. Elisha is clear, that the king had defined the level of his blessing by the number of arrows he had shot through the window. Had he shot more, his enemy would have been completely destroyed.

What has this got to do with sowing and reaping?

If a farmer is looking to harvest 2 tons of wheat, there will be a certain amount of seed he must sow in order to achieve that level of harvest.

In the same way, when we are sowing for provision, we already know what we want the harvest to look like. Like the farmer, there will be an amount of seed you will need to sow in order to realise that harvest.

So as we have seen in the accounts of the fishing

expedition, the widow's oil and the king, we can limit the level of our blessings by our own actions. In the same way, if we do not sow the right amount of seed, we can limit our blessings. Therefore it is really important when sowing a seed for provision that you listen carefully to God to tell you what you should sow.

My wife and I have a principle that we each listen to God for a number. Most of the time we entirely agree first time. However, if we hear different numbers, we go for the higher of the two numbers.

Filling in the table

So once you have heard from God about what or how much to sow for your provision, fill in columns 1 (Date sown) and 2 (Amount).

Prayer

"Father, please guide me as to how much to sow and where to sow my seed"

Day 36 - Sowing and Reaping (Part 5 - thankfulness)

"If an unbeliever invites you to a meal and you want to go, eat whatever is put before you without raising questions of conscience. But if someone says to you, "This has been offered in sacrifice," then do not eat it, both for the sake of the one who told you and for the sake of conscience. I am referring to the other person's conscience, not yours. For why is my freedom being judged by another's conscience? If I take part in the meal with thankfulness, why am I denounced because of something I thank God for?"
1 Cor 10

The third stage of the process for provision is giving thanks.

The verse in 1 Corinthians 10 above is interesting and contains some important principles. What Paul is saying is that if an unbeliever invites you to eat with them, you should eat anything put before you. However, if the host says "this has been offered in sacrifice" (or in other words, this has been offered to false gods or demons) you should not eat it. The reason you should not eat it is because of the message you are sending to the host. If the host sees you eating food which he has told you is dedicated to demons, he will believe there is nothing wrong with what he is doing.

Paul then expands on this explanation. He says "*I am referring to the other person's conscience, not yours. For why is my freedom being judged by another's conscience? If I take part in the meal with thankfulness, why am I denounced because of something I thank God for?*"

What Paul is saying is that the fact that someone tells you that the food has been dedicated to demons should not (apart from the impact on the conscience of the host) have any concerns for a believer. He then says "*If I take part in the meal with __thankfulness__, why I am denounced because of something I __thank__ God for?*" Paul is drawing attention to the power of thankfulness.

Paul is not suggesting you eat food dedicated to demons without doing anything first. The spiritual power of eating food sacrificed to idols was shown in the Old Testament, an example would be Numbers 25:3: *"The people ate the sacrificial meal and bowed down before these gods. So Israel yoked themselves to the Baal of Peor. And the Lord's anger burned against them."* Participating in food offered to idols led to idolatry and yoked the people of Israel to Baal of Peor (a demonic power).

Instead, Paul says that he can eat the food dedicated to demons if he first gives thanks for it first. This suggests that thankfulness is an incredibly powerful tool in the believer's life. But what does thankfulness actually do?

Thankfulness Dedicates Things and Situations to God

In 1 Tim 3:4 we read *"For everything God created is good, and nothing is to be rejected if it is received with __thanksgiving__, because it is consecrated by the word of God and prayer."* The effect of thanksgiving is to consecrate or to dedicate whatever we give to God. Thanksgiving restores things and situations to their original purpose.

Everything that God created is good. So the food that was created by God is good by design. However, taking something that is good and offering it to demons means that it is being taken outside its original purpose. Yet thankfulness consecrates that food back to God and thus restores it to its original purpose. Thus, what we give thanks for is given back to God so that it is good again.

Thankfulness Cleanses

Not only does thankfulness dedicate things to God, but it also cleanses it and makes it safe. Thus the dangers of food sacrificed to idols is avoided by giving thanks for it.

Thankfulness is for Every Situation

In Phil 4:6 we read *"Do not be anxious about anything, but in every situation, by* prayer and petition, with thanksgiving, present your requests to God." Paul who wrote this passage is making it clear that "in every situation" we are to employ the powerful tool of "thanksgiving". In fact, every time we make a request to God it should be accompanied by thanksgiving.

How does this apply to us?

When we sow a seed we give thanks for the seed. This sets the seed aside for God (or dedicates) the seed. Giving thanks for the seed makes it "good". It means that it can be used by God for His purposes. This is why Jesus gave thanks for the loaves and fishes before seeing the miracle of provision. Giving thanks dedicated the loaves and the fish to God so that He could perform a miracle of provision.

We also combine our request for provision with thanks. This is because thanksgiving is to accompany any prayers or requests for provision. We give thanks before we have actually received the provision.

Prayer

"May all of my prayers be accompanied by thanksgiving. May I see the power of thanksgiving in my life"

Day 37 - Sowing and Reaping (Part 6 - Believe before you receive/work of your hands)

"Therefore I say to you, whatever things you ask <u>when you pray, believe that you receive them,</u> and you will have them"
Mark 11:24

Believe before you receive

I mentioned yesterday that you give thanks before you receive your provision. Why did I say that? The bible is clear that we are to believe that we have received our provision **when** we pray. This is not when we receive what we have asked for, but instead when we ask.

So if you are asking God for a new washing machine, you are to believe that you have received it the moment you pray for it. In our process, the moment you have sowed for your provision you are to believe that you have received that provision.

You will see in Mark 11:24 that in order to obtain the things you have prayed for you need to believe the moment you pray. This should not be a shock for you. On day 28 we considered how we must partake in the divine nature in order to access the promises of God. We looked at Romans 4:17 which in referring to Abraham, says *"As it is written: "I have made you a father of many nations." He is our father in the sight of God, in whom he believed—the God who gives life to the dead **and calls into being things that were not.**"* God's nature is to call things into being that "were not".

In order to access the provision of God, we must call things into being that are not. In order to call things into being, we must first believe that we have received those things.

Practical Application

When filling out your seed table column 4 is labelled "date received". This should be filled in with the same date as you sowed your seed. This is a reminder to you that you believed that you received at the same time as you asked for provision.

God Blesses the Work of Your Hands

It is important to realise that God is not into lottery wins or money simply falling into your hands. God wants to bless the work of your hands and bring you provision in that manner. I set out on day 31 the ways in which God brings provision to you. You need to keep your eyes open for that provision.

From personal experience, I have received provision via insurance pay outs, through tax rebates, through bonus payments, through anonymous gifts, increases in investments and through savings I found in my household bills. Yet it is not only the money that you need to look out for, it is also the opportunities for that provision.

By means of an example, one of things I had sowed for was a set of De Walt power tools. I was often borrowing tools from my friends in the church for household tasks and wanted a set of my own. Note that I specifically told God the make of the tools I wanted. About 6 weeks after sowing my seed, I was browsing on the internet and saw that Amazon were offering the tool set I had sowed for and it was on a special offer on Amazon Prime day. They cost 60% of the normal retail price and I had enough money to afford these tools.

Now for those who don't know, Amazon Prime day was a one day event where Amazon offered special deals on the sale items. However, there were a limited number of each of the sale items and it was on a first come and first served basis. I knew from the internet that the tool set would be available from 6.00 pm that evening. I therefore prepared my computer ready to buy them the moment it hit 6 pm. As soon as the items became available I clicked on them to add them to my basket. Before I could pay for these items, I received a message that they had all been purchased. The message said that if someone failed to pay for them within 20 minutes, then these items would be offered to the next person in the queue. I checked the internet to see if this happened very often and the results were not promising.

I was gutted. I rang my wife and complained about the fact that my harvest had been stolen. My wife put me straight! She simply reminded me that I was standing in faith for these items. I had sowed a seed, I had believed before I had received them and so what had changed? Wives have a way of pointing out the truth. I therefore declared that the Lord had indeed set aside provision for me and declared out loud that I would be able to buy these tools at this cut price. Sure enough 5 minutes after that declaration, I had a message that the tools were available for me. I am now the proud owner of a set of good quality power tools which have proved invaluable for all sorts of DIY tasks.

What is the point of this story. God wants you to be involved in hunting out your harvest. He will work with you and guide you to the harvest. Therefore as soon as you have sown for your provision, keep your eyes open for how God will provide for you.

Prayer

"Father, as I sow, may I have the faith to believe before I receive. Also, guide me on my hunt for provision"

Day 38 - Sowing and Reaping (Part 7 - Putting it all together)

"Let us not become weary in doing good, for at the proper time we will reap a harvest if we do not give up. Therefore, as we have opportunity, let us do good to all people, especially to those who belong to the family of believers".
Gal 6:9

Now we have explored the individual parts of the sowing and reaping process, let's put them together.

I set out below a couple of examples of what we have sowed for. I shall take you through the process for each one of them.

Date Sown	Amount	Seed Name	Date Received	Date We Have It	Give Thanks
5/6/2016	£100	For the Garden shed we saw in Costco	5/6/2016	23/6/2016	Yes
May 2016	£10	New shoe cupboard	When sown	Received on 12/6/2016	Yes
22/6/2016	20 p	My daughter to be on the star	22/6/2016	Received on 28/6/2016	Yes

Example 1

The first item on the list was a garden shed. For a while we had been keeping our garden equipment in a small plastic mini-shed. The roof of this mini-shed had blown off during a winter storm and all of the electrical tools had been damaged and the metal tools had started to rust. My wife and I had spotted a shed we wanted at Costco. However, it was around £800 and at the time we had not got that money to spare to buy a new shed.

So we sowed a seed of £100 on 5 June 2016. We asked God for guidance as to how much to sow. We sowed it into our local church and recorded the description of the seed, how much we sowed and the date sown. We also stated in faith that we had received the shed on 5 June 2016.

It was just over 2 weeks later that we received our harvest. As part of an insurance claim, the insurers said that they could give us a larger sum of money by means of compensation if we took the payment in Argos vouchers (vouchers for a specific shop). I looked at the Argos catalogue to see if it was worth taking the vouchers. Amazingly, exactly the same shed as we saw in Costco was being sold by Argos and the amount of vouchers we received covered the entire cost.

We gave thanks to God for His provision.

Example 2

The second item on our list was a new shoe cupboard to put in our hallway. I must say that this was definitely my wife's choice as I always thought the area in front of the door was the ideal place to store shoes. However, I agreed that we could sow for a shoe cupboard.

We sowed our seed in May 2016. We sowed £10 (again after asking God). Again, I think we sowed this into our local church. We simply recorded that we believed God for provision on the date we sowed the seed. It was a few weeks later that we were blessed with an anonymous gift which precisely covered the shoe cupboard. We then purchased it and gave thanks.

Example 3

This is my favourite example of God's provision! Mainly because this is my daughter's testimony. My daughter and I were talking before she went to sleep at night. I asked her, what do you want from God more than anything. She said "Daddy, I want to be on the star". I asked her "what does that mean?" She replied "If you are really good in class you go onto the star. I have been really good all the time but, my teacher has never put me on the star."

"Ok" I replied. "This is what we are going to do…". I then told her about the power of sowing and reaping. I said we are going to trust Jesus to put you on the star. I asked her how much she wanted to sow. She replied "I don't know £10?". I had heard clearly from God that the sum should be 20p. So I said to my daughter, 'I believe the Lord said 20 pence". So she got 20 pence out of her money box and gave it to me. I made an online payment at that time to the church of 20 pence (goodness knows what the church accountant will make of that!).

We then held hands together and declared that we were sowing the 20 pence for her to be on the star. I then recorded the seed for her in the table.

Six days later, my daughter's normal teacher was not taking the class. Instead the deputy headmistress was taking the class. Sure enough, she recognised my daughter's good behaviour and put her on the star. I was so excited at God's goodness. I was so much more excited for this breakthrough than for my own provision. God had demonstrated his faithfulness to my daughter and was building a foundation in her life that will last her a lifetime!

Conclusion

I hope that the examples above have given you an idea and encouragement to start sowing and reaping for your provision. These are only limited examples and we have several pages of seeds we have sown and seen God provide for.

Prayer

"Father, may I trust you with my provision. Please bless the seed that I sow"

Section 4 - Principles for Increase

Day 39 - Increase comes from ability

*"Again, it will be like a man going on a journey, who called his servants and entrusted his wealth to them. To one he gave five bags of gold, to another two bags, and to another one bag, **each according to his ability**." Matt 25:14-15*

For our final two days, we are going to explore the principles for increase. That is if you want to be trusted with a larger money assignment from God, what attitudes and abilities do you need to demonstrate?

The parable of the talents as recorded in Matthew 25 gives us guidance as to how God allocates His money assignments. In the parable, the wealthy man or master represents God. The servants represent us.

Each servant was given a money assignment. In the same way each of us is given a money assignment from God. The important thing to note is that the master in the parable gave the servants a money assignment in accordance with "their ability". So in short, those servants who were most able to handle money were given a larger money assignment than those who were given less.

This is the same for us. God gives us a money assignment in proportion to our ability to handle that assignment. If we want to be trusted with a larger money assignment, our starting point must be to increase our ability to handle money well.

Key 1 - Steward What You Currently Have Well

The starting point for increase is handling what you currently have as well as you possibly can. The servants in the parable were required to take the money they had and see increase in that money.

We have a similar assignment. As discussed in previous days, our mission is to take our money and pursue our primary purpose of giving to His kingdom to see it expand. The increase we are required to show is an increase in God's kingdom.

In order to do this we must discern between what is bread for eating (or money for spending on ourselves) and what is seed for sowing (money to give away). We are to employ the principles of wisdom so that we are accountable for every £1 that God has given us to manage. We are also to be living in faith for our provision.

Let's take an example to make this point clearer. There are two people: Mr Spender and Mr Giver. Both Mr Spender and Mr Giver get paid the same amount of money. Mr Spender takes all of his money and spends it on himself buying himself the latest clothes and gadgets. Mr Giver takes 10% and pays his tithe. He takes another 10% and gives it away as offerings. He then spends the other 80% on himself.

If you were God, who would you trust with a larger money assignment? It is obvious isn't it? You would give it to the person who is supporting your wife (the church is described as the wife of God) through their tithe and is expanding your kingdom through generosity.

When counselling people with very little money, I always try to establish the tithe. I know that this is often the key to increase in their life. When the tithe is established, God quickly moves to bring them increase in supernatural ways.

Yet your money assignment cannot be separated from your work assignment or even your church assignment. We try to separate and compartmentalise our lives into different areas. God does not do this. A bad attitude at work tends to stem from a heart attitude which needs adjusting.

So we are to show hard work and honesty in every sphere of our lives. We are to work in our jobs and engage in our churches as if we were serving God directly. Many people can miss their opportunity for increase because they do not realise that serving their bosses at work is a spiritual principle and a test.

Key 2 - Embrace Change

In order to be trusted with a larger money assignment, you have to change.

Let me give you an example to explain what I mean. Let us say you are running a lemonade stand in your driveway. In order to do this you are required to buy lemons, sugar and water and make the lemonade. You then have to sell the lemonade.

Now say you are running Coca Cola. Whilst the basic principles are the same, you have to gather ingredients and mix them together and sell them, there are a lot more complications! You need premises to make the drinks in the massive quantities that are required. You need distribution networks to deliver the products over the entire world. You need advertising and media relation people. You need to engage in tax and regulatory laws all over the world. You need to employ thousands of people to run the company. The skills and knowhow you need to run Coca Cola are so much greater than those required to run a lemonade stall.

Yet many of us don't realise that in order to be trusted with a larger money assignment, you will have to change the way you operate. It is not that what you are doing now is wrong, simply that more money will require new skills.

Firstly you will need new structures. The more money you get to manage, the more organised you will need to be in order to effectively manage that money. You need to put in place structures in order to manage that money.

Secondly you will need new ways of working. No longer can you do everything. You will need to learn how to delegate to others. You may have increased demands on your time and may need to employ people to do jobs for you.

Thirdly you will need new people skills. The greater your money assignment, the more demands will be placed on your time. Also the types of people you interact with may also change. You will need to acquire new people skills.

Fourthly, priorities will need to considered and changed. How you spend your time and what should you spend your time doing must be challenged. What is important and how do you protect your time also needs to be considered.

Conclusion

Take time now to consider how you can better manage your current money assignment. Also consider what you will need to change in order to handle a larger money assignment. Consider what skills that will involve and make plans now for how you can acquire those skills. Read books or go on courses in the areas you need help in. If possible use resources from believers who have tapped into kingdom principles of how to do these things.

Prayer

"Father, I would like to be trusted with a larger money assignment. Please give me wisdom to manage my current assignment well and prepare me for increase"

Day 40 - Heart Attitude

"And everyone who has left houses or brothers or sisters or father or mother or wife or children or fields for my sake will receive a hundred times as much and will inherit eternal life. But many who are first will be last, and many who are last will be first.

"For the kingdom of heaven is like a landowner who went out early in the morning to hire workers for his vineyard. He agreed to pay them a denarius for the day and sent them into his vineyard.

"About nine in the morning he went out and saw others standing in the marketplace doing nothing. He told them, 'You also go and work in my vineyard, and I will pay you whatever is right.' So they went.

"He went out again about noon and about three in the afternoon and did the same thing. About five in the afternoon he went out and found still others standing around. He asked them, 'Why have you been standing here all day long doing nothing?'

"'Because no one has hired us,' they answered.
"He said to them, 'You also go and work in my vineyard.'
"When evening came, the owner of the vineyard said to his foreman, 'Call the workers and pay them their wages, beginning with the last ones hired and going on to the first.'

"The workers who were hired about five in the afternoon came and each received a denarius. So when those came who were hired first, they expected to receive more. But each one of them also received a denarius. When they received it, they began to grumble against the landowner. 'These who were hired last worked only one hour,' they said, 'and you have made them equal to us who have borne the burden of the work and the heat of the day.'
"But he answered one of them, 'I am not being unfair to you, friend. Didn't you agree to work for a denarius? Take your pay and go. I want to give the one who was hired last the same as I gave you. Don't I have the right to do what I want with my own money? Or are you envious because I am

generous?'
"So the last will be first, and the first will be last."" Matt
19:29 - 20:16

I have quoted a longer passage of scripture today, but please take time to read it carefully. It contains an incredibly important principle for biblical increase.

Jesus starts with a promise in chapter 19. He says that *"And everyone who has left houses or brothers or sisters or father or mother or wife or children or fields for my sake will receive a hundred times as much and will inherit eternal life."*

What Jesus is promising is that anyone who has given up houses (material possessions), family, or fields (or the means of acquiring wealth) will receive 100 times as much and will inherit eternal life. Other accounts of this verse say they will receive 100 times in this earth and in heaven. So the promise is huge increase in this lifetime if you give generously. As such there is a key here to increase in your money assignment.

Yet after this promise Jesus says *"But many who are first will be last, and many who are last will be first."* The use of the word "but" is critical. If I say to you "I promise to buy you an ice cream but you must clean your car", what I am in fact saying is "if you clean your car, I will buy you an ice cream". In the same way Jesus is qualifying the promise of increase with this phrase *"many who are first will be last, and many who are last will be first".* So the promise of 100 fold increase is subject to the principle that the first will be last.

What does this phrase mean? Jesus explains what he means by this phrase in chapter 20 by means of a parable. We know that he is explaining this phrase in the parable because concludes the parable in verse 16 of chapter 20 by saying *"so the last will be first and the first will be last".*

What does this parable mean? Let us break it down into parts:

1.   **The Landowner -** this represents God.

2. **The Workers** - these represent us.

The workers are all employed at different times by the landowner. In the same way we all receive assignments from God at different times. I may have been called to serve God in the local church for 20 years, but someone else only for 6 months.

Yet when it came to being paid, the landowner chose to pay those who had worked for a short period of time first. Why did he do this? The obvious reason is so that those who had been working longest would see him do it!

What did he pay those who had worked for a short period of time? He paid them what he had agreed to pay for those who had worked all day. He therefore chose to be generous and reward these people beyond what they deserved.

For those who had been working all day, they expected to be paid more than those who had only worked for a short period of time. They were therefore upset when they only got what they had agreed to be paid. The landowner asked them "*are you envious because I am generous*".

Applying this to us, when we work for God we may receive our fair wages or we may receive extravagant generosity. Your fellow worker may receive fair wages or they may receive extravagant generosity. This is simply the way God works. He is at minimum fair but he is also generous. There will be times when you receive a fair wage and at other times you will receive generosity.

God is looking to test your heart when you see others receiving generosity whilst you get a fair wage. We can either be like the workers in the parable and have a sense of entitlement or alternatively accept that God is generous and if he wants to bless others He is allowed to do so. A sense of entitlement is ugly. It looks at everyone else and compares yourself to them. It demands a level of treatment which is in keeping with your efforts and skills.

When Jesus is saying the first will be last and the last will be first, what he is saying is that if we can lose our sense of entitlement when others are being treated generously, we will qualify to be first. If we however, demand to be first due to our entitlement, we will be last.

In other words, the promise of 100 times increase in this earth is subject to you having a correct attitude to entitlement. God can only trust you with 100 times blessings if your heart is able to celebrate the blessings of others without becoming envious and having a sense of entitlement. Let me be clear, you do not deserve 100 times blessings, this is God's radical generosity. So in order to receive the blessings of 100 times blessings, you must be able to celebrate other people's blessings without becoming resentful.

This is a test of your heart. God can only trust blessings to those who have a healthy heart.

Prayer

"Father, give me a heart that celebrates the blessings of others. Qualify me for my own increase"

Appendix 1
Current Monthly Budget

Income	Amount (£)	Possible Saving + Why/ Setting budget
Person 1 (after tax)		
Person 2		
State Pension		
Private Pension/Annuity		
Benefits		
Income from Savings/ Investments		
Gifts from family/friends		
TOTAL INCOME		
EXPENSES		
Expenses - Home		
Mobile Phone		
TV Licence		
Internet		
Home Phone		
Garden Maintenance		
Oil (home fuel)		
Electricity		
Gas		
Water		
Council Tax		
Overdraft Costs		
Bank account fee		
Home insurance		
Mortgage/Rent		
Plumbing/Boiler cover		
Mortgage Life insurance		

Income	Amount (£)	Possible Saving + Why/ Setting budget
Mortgage Payment Protection		
Life insurance		
Food and household shopping		
Expenses - Travel		
Car Tax		
Parking		
Car Insurance		
Expenses - Travel		
Rail/Bus/Taxi/Tube		
Breakdown Cover		
Expenses - Debts		
Credit Card Repayments		
Hire Purchase repayments		
Personal Loan Repayments		
Car Loan Repayments		
Expenses - Family		
Pet food		
School Trips		
Pocket Money		
Laundry/Dry Cleaning		
Children's Travel		
Baby-Sitting		
Childcare/Playgroups		
Pet Insurance		
Travel Insurance		
Expenses - Entertainment		
Satellite/Digital TV		
Family Days Out		
Cinema/Theatre Trips		

Income	Amount (£)	Possible Saving + Why/ Setting budget
Books/Music/Films/ Computers		
Big days out		
Shopping for fun		
Pet Costs		
Hobbies		
IT/Computing (antivirus etc)		
DVD Rental/film rental		
Drinking out		
Eating Out		
Expenses - Clothes, Health and Beauty		
Optical Bills		
Haircuts		
Dentistry		
Beauty Treatments		
Healthcare Cash Plans		
Dental Insurance		
Private Medical Insurance		
Fitness/Sports/Gym		
New Clothes		
Expenses - Education and Courses		
University Tuition Fees		
School Fees		
Your courses		
Expenses - other		
Newspapers and magazines		
Meals at work		
Cigarettes/Cigars etc.		

Income	Amount (£)	Possible Saving + Why/ Setting budget
Coffee/Sandwiches/ Snacks		
GIVING		
Tithe		
Offerings		
Charitable Donations		
TOTAL EXPENSES		
Budget Deficit/surplus		

Appendix 2 - Debt Sheet

DEBT	Name	Outstanding Balance	Rate of Interest
CREDIT CARDS			
LOANS - including catalogue credit, mortgage etc.			
HIRE PURCHASE			
FAMILY LOANS			
OUTSTANDING BILLS			

Appendix 3 - Debt Repayments

Date	Which Debt	Amount Repaid	Outstanding Balance	How much money is saved (then used to increase debt repayments)

Date	Which Debt	Amount Repaid	Outstanding Balance	How much money is saved (then used to increase debt repayments)

Appendix 4 - Summary of Wisdom Steps

1. Work out what you are currently spending (Appendix 1)

2. Find savings

3. Set limits and create your envelopes

4. Establish your tithe

5. Sell goods to create a lump sum

6. Use the lump sum to pay down debts to create more cash low

7. Create emergency savings pot

8. Pay down debts as quickly as possible

9. Increase investment, savings and offerings

10. Set new targets for your spending, saving, offerings and investment.

Appendix 5 - Seed Table

Date Sown	Amount	Seed Name	Date Received	Date We Have It	Give Thanks

Date Sown	Amount	Seed Name	Date Received	Date We Have It	Give Thanks

Appendix 6 - Testimonies

These are testimonies of a number of people who have either attended courses (called the Money Revolution) which reflect the principles in this book or have read the book and applied the principles.

Lorraine's Testimony

"The Money Revolution Course [which was a course which birthed this book] has transformed the way I view my finances.

I have had an issue with most prosperity teachings in the past, but Clive's work focuses on God's heart and our purpose in this area before anything else. Due to this perspective, I received it wholeheartedly with more revelation than expected.

What stood out for me in the first few lessons was that I had a limited, worldly view of my finances and my contribution to the kingdom of God (due to part time employment and having young kids).

Also the lesson on how to (or not to) pray for increase was a revelation.

At a more basic level I am a much better steward of my finances and my improved communication with my husband in this area has blessed our marriage.

Being the practical person that I am; I applied the principles straight away and I received an 18% increase in my salary within the following month! A few weeks after that I won an award which allowed me to complete a course of my choice with all expenses paid up to ten thousand pounds!

It's great to receive a more comfortable income, but also it blesses me to know that my increase advances God's kingdom.

God has blessed Clive with wonderful insight in this area and I would encourage others to receive it and be blessed also."

Liz's Testimony

"Thank you very much again for the Money Revolution course. Look forward to reading the book!

So I would say as a testimony of doing the course.

I learnt so much doing this comprehensive course and I am still implementing some of the things. It is a like a tool kit which I can refer back to, study and apply.

One of the key things you taught us was to act on the revelation we received from the lessons. The power of acting on what we hear before logic and analysis take over. Some of the things were new, other things gave me greater clarity to know how to put them practically in my life. From the practical application of the course, I found around £110 pounds a month from savings in different areas, by changing my energy supplier, my bank, and mobile phone to SIM only.

The course gave me the impetus to give a lot more thought to what I was using my money for. Some areas I have increased my spending, in other areas I have been more careful.

Clive, is a brilliant teacher, he explains things very clearly and uses familiar bible parables and bible passages with fresh insight and personal testimonies to demonstrate how to use faith and wisdom. For example, from the feeding of the five thousand the importance of picking up the leftovers and applying that to things like meal planning.

Before money comes to me now, I can make decisions about how I will use it wisely to maximise what I can give and what I will use. He gives hope for change by applying faith to apparently impossible situations. I sowed for a plane ticket and secured one for virtually half price by stepping out in faith and acting on what I heard in the class and what I heard in my spirit to do. Above, all he lives what he teaches and I would recommend this to everyone."

Bonny's Testimony

"I would like to thank God for the teaching the Lord has given Clive for the Money Revolution course. What an eye opener! To know that we are stewards of God's resources and that increase comes through improved management of 'His' resources.

As a result of the teaching, I have begun to better manage my finances through planning. I continue to tithe and give offerings and sow as the Lord leads. I have started seeing an increase in my finances coming from my second stream of income. I have also started to be better aware of managing my time so I can see increase in other areas of my life."

Sharon's Testimony

""Money revolution, what's going to be different about this one?", I thought. You see I have done a few money workshops before and although I do not doubt what is being said I just can't seem to get this money thing. It seems to be the biggest hurdle that I have yet to overcome. What is the problem? I give I'm not stingy or am I?

My consistency in giving tithes and offerings has been an issue my whole Christian walk. Nonetheless, I trust Clive and Caroline [his wife], and have seen God bless them abundantly and when I say abundantly I don't just mean in material gain. I have seen God move within their family affairs in such a mighty way.

Caroline has been a long term friend of mine and over the course of the years prior to this Money Revolution course, Caroline would say "make sure you give your tithes and offerings - it is a key to blessing". ARGHHH. I just couldn't get it. It sounded like I was buying things from God - SURELY NOT!

Now the enemy loved my thoughts he'd chip in "it's down to Clive's job, come on he's a solicitor" and he would add "look at his upbringing as a sound good Christian boy from a good Christian family - he's the reason why their children are now stable". These thoughts would rule my mind for a time, but I knew there was more to it. I have seen God move in such ways in their life so that it was clear that it was not just Clive's job or background that was the source of the blessing - it had to be God.

Anyway, as a parent who is walking alone, I was always counting the pennies. I would tithe for months and then something would be needed. As I would have no emergency fund, my tithing was sacrificed and my consistency was gone. Then it would be weeks again and the same cycle would occur. In this whole time the devil would be having a field day, telling me "I'm never going to amount to anything", "I'm always going to be scraping the bottom of the barrel", "I can't even give consistently- a simple Christian principle and as usual I can't keep it up."

Ahhhh it was "doing my head in" because if there is anything I know about Clive and Caroline, it's that they are faithful to God. They practice what they preach, and above all their heart was for me to be free and walk in the abundance that God had for me. I KNOW THIS, so why am I struggling?

So, back to the MONEY REVOLUTION course - I put my name down and begin the course. The course begins and I'm taking in each week some key nuggets that Clive is now sharing, one is that when he has a sense that the money he has is having a greater hold over him than it should, he gives it away. Ok, one for me, so I now have this practice down to a tee. Not that I have a lot of money, but thought ok I'm got to start somewhere.

As we went through each week I'm beginning to see that it's not the amount of money and it's not about buying things from God, it's your heart. Anyway, WEEK FIVE was the game changer for me, I had missed the session but with God nothing is missed. The sessions were being recorded. So that week I started to listen to week five and Clive starts to speak about what lie have we believing about finance [Note these lessons are found on days 10 and 11 of this book]. OH, this is a bit different, a bit deep. Ok I can feel myself welling up inside, so I turn off the tape.

As I carried on my daily chores, I could hear the spirit prompting me to sit down and listen to the tape again. I avoided it that day and the next day but the spirit was still prompting me. Ok, so I sit down and listen to the whole tape crying. I write down the lies that I had been listening to me whole life. Things from my grandmother to my mother. I realised that I was always watching all the woman in my family counting the pennies and paying for everything, just barely keeping things going. I had believed that this is how I would be and sure enough this is how it had been up until that day. But God broke something in the spirit and I was suddenly awakened to the truth of what God was saying to me.

As the weeks progressed we spoke on what God's heart is for His children (ME) and how His plan had always been to bless me with more than I could ever imagine or think. We spoke of the lie and God's truth. And then we spoke of sowing and reaping. Now this is something I know is biblical but it still did not feel right buying things from God. Anyway, slowly as I looked more into God's word on sowing and reaping it began to make sense. So I had determined in my heart to pursue this sowing and reaping.

Clive challenged us to write down things that we desired and then pray about it, we then ask God: first how much we should sow; and then where we should sow. Now what I liked about this session is that Clive, having great insight, understood that the enemy may hold us up by saying we don't know where to sow. So, Clive gave us a tip, look to sow into the Church if you have not been directed specifically by God. "Ok" I thought - good Christian answer! I understood the principle of giving tithes and offerings, but this was sowing for what I wanted - this felt different. This was a struggle for me - am I allowed to sow into things that I want? It was only because I know Clive and I know his heart is for me and others to prosper, I'm like "ok I'm going to give this sowing malarkey a go".

So I pray to God because I desperately needed a bed. I had just recently moved into my new house and I did not have a bed (I was actually sleeping on the sofa). I was only on benefits and did not have sufficient income to afford a bed. So I pray and God says to me sow £50. £50 - God really!

I didn't think I had even £10 spare never mind £50, anyway I knew I had heard God and decided to do this. I went to the bank on Friday (7 June) and there was an extra £80 pounds in my account over what I thought I had. "Great", I thought. I have now got the £50 that God has told me to sow. Come the Saturday I was low on food and my old way is to go out and just spend any extra money to buy food or what I think we need.

No no no! I'm now in a battle with myself. Anyway, I take the £50 and I put it in an envelope and record that I am sowing for my bed. I have a battle getting to church on the Sunday, but I get there (my big kid's playing up). I put the envelope the offering as quickly as I can so I can shut up the devil.

Anyway, the last Saturday of the teaching comes on Saturday the 15th June and I'm leaving to go to my parents. Suddenly a lady from the church hands me an envelope and I put it in my bag and off I go to my parents. I get to my parent's house and then look in the envelope and there is £200 pounds. I was so excited. What a blessing as this is going towards my bed. Now, God had not finished there. My mum, who did not know I did not have a bed yet, tells me that she has picked out a bed for me and rings to ask what colour I wanted. I told her and she sent me a picture of the bed that I had been looking at. I said it was lovely and before I could say anything else I got a text to say that she had bought it and it was coming to mine the next week.

WOW. Now I praised God I had never owned a new bed in my life it had always been second-hand. I now have a new bed and then God said "use the £200 I gave you because I want you to go and buy yourself new quilt, pillows, covers and all that your new bed needs". I was on the floor. God loves me so much that He knew all I had owned up until then had been second-hand and now He was showing me that He wants me to have new things. It's not just that it is new but it's that He values me so much. Just as a husband values his wife, God wants me to be happy and safe and secure in Him.

I then sowed for my last year university fees and they are now paid. Not only were they paid, but the bursar found me and filled in the bursary form for me sent it off and then found me again and told me it was paid in full.

God also has told me to keep sowing and to sow into marriages in money and prayer. I am still sowing today. As a result, I have had my rent arrears paid off. I have had my credit card paid off. I now have no catalogue bills and I'm now working on my overdraft and will have repaid this in full by March of next year.

I really do believe that God is showing me what a husband looks like. Through my giving and sowing He is showing me that He is truly is my provider. Thank you Clive and Caroline for allowing me access to your lives and for continually loving me (a challenge I know). May god continue to bless and use you both, forever in my prayers."

Louise's Testimony

"I was listening to the lesson around naming the seed you are sowing. The Lord has on many occasions has told me what to give. One day, I was reviewing my giving. I was tithing and giving to missions but had never named the seed.

We were asked by Clive to write down the seed we wanted to sow. One of mine was for my daughter, who was so unhappy in her retail job. She wanted out, she was constantly being called to answer to management. She commented that quite a few people were leaving the company. Indeed one of the managers was setting people up to fail. The atmosphere was incredibly hostile. For weeks, call after call, she was expressing to me how she doubted her own abilities.

So I named that seed and gave it in an offering on Sunday. My daughter told me that she was taking a week of holiday from work and at the same time she was going to look and apply to any job suitable for her. By that Thursday, she called having had a phone interview for a job which involved working with people with learning disabilities.

The feedback she received from that phone interview was extremely positive. A face to face interview was set up for the next day. She was so excited. They asked if there were

6 more like her. Wow! What confidence. The following Tuesday she was greeted by one of the clients with learning disabilities living in the house.

The Manager came out to see my daughter and said "I have heard such a lot about you. What would you like full time or part time".

She went from worthless to worthwhile, from under to on top of. From devalued to valued. She has passed her final written assessment with an impressive score of 93% and is now a Support Worker for a major charity!"

.